Bologna

Footprint

Ben Donald

Contents

Listings

About the author

Ben Donald is a freelance travel writer whose journalism has appeared in the (London) *Times* and various travel magazines, such as *Traveller*, *Global Adventure* and *Travel Africa*. He is a keen independent traveller, fluent in a number of languages, including Italian, and has lived and worked in several countries. During a year in Turin he really got under the skin of the Italian culture and all its beautiful and frustrating paradoxes. He is the author of Footprint's pocket guide to Turin and co-author of the *Book of Cities* (Pavilion, 2004)

Acknowledgements

I would like to thank: Ali at TalkaBOut for having her finger on the pulse and particularly in researching the bars and clubs section; my mate Chris at Hotel Spira for his unflagging and spontaneous hospitality and for his companionship in researching the best restaurants, bars and clubs for you; and lastly, Merida, for putting up with the many absences during my research and all the lonely evenings while I transformed my notes into this book.

For the second edition, my thanks also go to Giorgia Zabbini at the Bologna tourist office for her invaluable insight into all the latest developments in the city.

With streets like embroidered cloth, threaded with the arches of continuous colonnades, the heart of Bologna is a giant cloister. Under processions of classical columns and in the shadows cast between the half-moons of its winding alleys, the city inspires a furtive combination of intimacy and wandering, revealing her secrets to the unhurried visitor prepared to be led astray. Above and behind its chiaroscuro porticoes, Bologna is a rose-red city of bombastic churches and vainglorious palaces, lasting testaments to the architectural flattery bestowed by the papal and civic forces that vied for control of the city. Striving for immortality, these patriarchs commissioned lavish chapels, frescoes and tombs, creating in the process one of the most influential schools of Italian art and bequeathing to the city a litter of monuments and masterpieces. These remain in good condition and accessible, not ominously *sotto restauro*, as elsewhere in Italy.

The learned and the red

Although all roads might lead to Rome, they almost certainly pass through Bologna on the way. On a plain between the Apennine Mountains and the Adriatic Coast, Bologna has always been a strategic city. But it was also the city's propensity for free thinking that invaders wanted to control. Bologna has always been the Italian residence of pioneering thought, earning it the soubriquet, Bologna *la dotta* (the learned). Around the same time as Bolognese physicist, Guglielmo Marconi, was discovering radio, Bologna became the birthplace and home of the Italian political Left. Already dubbed *la rossa* (the red) for its famed red buildings, Bologna's second nickname gained a more figurative meaning.

Raw ham and Ferraris

Bologna is the capital of Emilia-Romagna, a region of fertile plains, beautiful mountain scenery and a stretch of coastline that has long been a mecca for clubbers and sun-worshippers. It is also known for the cultural and material affluence of its other historic cities, such as Modena, Parma, Ferrara and Ravenna, and for the numerous Italian icons with which they have become synonymous: from Parmesan cheese and Parma ham to fast cars and fashion. Local brands, Ferrari and Furla, apparently reinforce the stereotypes of Italian boys and girls.

The fat of the land

The roar of engines, however, takes place mostly away from the ivory towers of the city – Bologna is a place for strolling and talking, if only to walk off one of the city's famous meals. The city is without doubt the stomach, if not the taste buds, of the country. The Bolognese have always taken the cultivation, preparation and consumption of their food very seriously, providing a very palatable edge to their socialism and earning the city its final affectionate appellation, Bologna *la grassa* (the fat).

At a glance

The heart of Bologna is still its Roman core, piazza Maggiore, at the confluence of the city's two main roads, via Ugo Bassi and via Rizzoli. These two roads are the contemporary face of the old Roman road, via Emilia, which once traversed the whole of the region. The area now referred to as the Centro Storico or old centre is defined by the *circonvallazione*: the busy main perimeter road which follows the line of the city's old extremity walls, joining up the 12 city gates.

Centre: piazza Maggiore and around

The pulse of the city and reference point for any visitor is its main square. Buffered at one end by the unfinished Gothic aspect of the Basilica di San Petronio and enclosed by the arcades and crenellations of squat edifices to Bologna's past prowess, this grandiose square is now a backdrop to a human theatre of poseurs and street artists. The perimeter of piazza Maggiore and the area beyond its eastern flanks called the Quadrilatero once constituted the entire extent of the original Roman settlement. The Quadrilatero is now a grid of teeming market streets full of colours, smells and bustle by day, and lively chic bars by night.

Northeast: the university quarter

Northeast of piazza Maggiore, down via Rizzoli and beyond the *due torri* (two towers) that have become the city's icon is the anarchic and bohemian atmosphere of via Zamboni and the heart of studentland. Along this street are the main faculty buildings and museums of Europe's oldest university and a dense concentration of bars and cafés under its porticoes. Returning west along via delle Belle Arti one finds La Pinacoteca, home to the largest collection of masterpieces by the Bolognese masters.

Tucked in, just north of via Rizzoli, are the sheer backalleys of Bologna's former Jewish ghetto, still redolent of the suspicion that reigned in the 1500s. Further north around via Piella and via Cattani are some of Bologna's less-visited streets, offering a slice of local working-class life and, in a sliver of the old underground waterway, a glimpse of the city's concealed past. Beyond them is piazza VIII Agosto and the Montagnola gardens, which come alive on Fridays and Saturdays, attracting crowds to the city's fleamarket. Returning south to piazza Maggiore along the main drag of via dell'Indipendenza is the city's cavernous cathedral.

Southeast: Santo Stefano and around
The three arteries of via Santo Stefano, via Castliglione and Strada Maggiore that lead southeast from piazza Maggiore make up the most tranquil and picturesque part of town. You can stroll up and down endless arcades enjoying the shifting perspectives of palatial buildings as they are framed by each arch. At their heart is the Santo Stefano complex of interconnecting churches, a maze of cloisters and chapels, each more intricate than the first.

Southwest: via d'Azeglio and via del Pratello
Leading due south from piazza Maggiore, the elegant via d'Azeglio and its capillaries are a catwalk where Bologna's glamourpusses and gatsbys prowl in search of the latest in chic from the city's alphabet of designer label stores. Further west, beyond the jagged edges of San Francesco church lies the seedy district of via del Pratello, Bologna's former red light district, whose concentration of late-night drinking dives and divers has earned it a popularity among those with a *nostalgie de la boue*.

Northwest: around via Galliera
Via dell'Indipendenza, Bologna's noisy main thoroughfare, bore the brunt of the Allied bombardments of the Second World War and, despite subsequent reconstruction, the area feels generally cold and angular though via Galliera has always been considered dark blue on the local Monopoly board. Hidden under via del Porto

and at Porta Lame are the docks, where goods from as far north as the Po arrived via the nearby river Reno and the city's network of canals. These redundant industrial spaces are being reclaimed by the city's youth and transformed into clubs and cultural centres, making this area, at night, one of Bologna's most genuinely urban.

Exhibition Centre and around

North of the old city centre in a dedicated trade fair zone you can find a statement of Bologna's eye to the future: a modern urban landscape of glass and aluminium in contrast to the city's predominantly classical lines. Bologna has a calendar of fairs for industries as varied as underwear, modern art and cars. Nearby is the Ducati factory and museum.

Hills to the south

Bologna lies in the lee of the Apennines, whose verdant foothills creep up to the south of the city, concealing rustic villages and extravagant villas in their undulations. Atop one such hill stands Bologna's guardian, the sanctuary of the Madonna di San Luca, connected to the city by a colonnade of 666 arches. Energetic pilgrims are rewarded with magnificent views of the red city below.

Around Bologna

Emilia-Romagna holds many treasures, from historic and cultural centres such as Ferrara, seat of the famous Este dynasty, and the Byzantine ruins of Ravenna to gastronomic wonders in the cheese-making factories of Parma and national parks in the Apennines, where you can trek, watch wildlife or ski. Automotive past and present can be seen at the famous Ferrari testing track and museum at Maranello near Modena or at the grand prix circuit at Imola. Or if you just want to chill out, why not head east and dip your toes in the Adriatic or take part in the national sport of sunbathing at one of the beaches around Rimini?

★ **Ten of the best**

Best

1 Basilica di San Petronio Unfinished façade and vast interior containing many chapels and an outsize sundial, p32.

2 Chiesa di Santo Stefano Complex of seven interwoven churches, adorned with fine art and enclosed within cloisters. One of the most tranquil spots in the city, p66.

3 Le Due Torri From the top of the Torre Asinelli, one of Bologna's iconic twin towers, enjoy breathtaking views over the city's rooftops and the surrounding countryside, p47.

4 La Pinacoteca Nazionale Superb collection of paintings by Bolognese masters and others, including Giotto, p58.

5 Portico and Santuario di San Luca Bologna's shrine on the hill is accessed by a continuous colonnade of 666 arches. The panoramic views are spectacular, p89.

6 San Giacomo Maggiore and l'Oratorio di Santa Cecilia One of Bologna's most elegant and significant churches, with the hidden treasure of a cycle of scenes by Costa, Francia and Aspertini, p52.

7 Chiesa di San Domenico A beautiful church famous for the *arca*, the ornate canopy for the tomb of St Dominic and for its many lavish chapels, p69.

8 Palazzo dell'Archiginnasio As counterpoint to all the churches, visit the starting point of Bologna's famous and ancient university, p41.

9 Il Quadrilatero and Il Mercato di Mezzo This ancient Roman grid of streets is a feast for the eyes and noses of those who have come to Bologna for its fabled food, p40.

10 La Sala Borsa Now developed into a child-friendly, fully interactive library and research point, Bologna's former stock exchange also contains some of the city's best Roman remains, not to say memories of the Bolognese who suffered at the hands of the fascist movement, p45.

Trip planner

Italy's climate makes it an attractive holiday or short-break proposition virtually all year round. However Bologna can get extremely hot between May and September and there can also be regular and spectacular downpours of rain, especially in spring and autumn. In both cases the city's arcades really come into their own for shelter and shade. If there is a bad time to visit, it is August when many of the city's museums, buildings and – worse still – restaurants close, sometimes for the whole month, sometimes just for the middle two weeks. All year round, visitors staying for a long weekend are advised to make the most of the weekend days as many sights, shops and restaurants close on a Monday. Many shops also close on Thursday afternoons.

A weekend (2-4 days)

Most of Bologna's main attractions are within a short walk of each other. However, there might be a temptation to cram in too many sights. Time is equally enjoyably spent simply strolling around the arcaded streets. That said, a weekend visit will comfortably allow for a snapshot of the principal sights in the heart of Bologna's old centre, while still allowing time for shopping and lounging in cafés. Starting in piazza Maggiore, look inside the Basilica di San Petronio and climb up the Torre Asinelli before wandering around the streets of the university quarter. Head down via Zamboni and into the beautiful church and oratory of San Giacomo Maggiore before ending up in the Pinacoteca gallery, the best introduction to the Bolognese school of art. If it is Friday or Saturday, the market on piazza VIII Agosto will make a lively antidote to the painting. You should also make time to look around the serene cloisters of the Santo Stefano church complex. Finally, you'll probably want to walk off all the *mortadella* by taking a Sunday stroll up the colonnade to the shrine of San Luca, where you can enjoy panoramic views over the city and lower Apennines.

→ Museum passes

A yearly pass (*abbonamento*), good value if you are staying for more than a weekend or plan to return, is €25 and allows unlimited access to Bologna's museums. Visitors staying for a shorter period might find the *biglietto cumulativo* (one- or three-day passes) better, costing €6 and €8 respectively. For €14 you can also buy a *biglietto integrato*, valid for three days and allowing you access to the museums and also use of public transport. For further information contact the Municipality **T** 051-203040, or the tourist hotline, **T** 051-246541, *Mon-Sat 0900-1900*.

One week or more

A week will give you time to enjoy the essential sights at a more leisurely pace and to linger in some of the city's interesting districts such as the Mirasoli at the end of via Castiglione, the via del Pratello and the canal area around via delle Moline. If you are particularly interested in Bologna's watery and underground past, you could visit the fascinating canals that go right under the city. You might also want to inspect the treasures of the Chiesa di San Domenico and the magical hidden Chiesa della Madonna del Colombano in via Parigi. The Jewish ghetto and the new Museo della Musica are also interesting historical diversions that will lay open the city. If you go up to the shrine at San Luca, the surrounding hills offer many lovely parks, monasteries and villas, such as Parco di Villa Ghigi and San Michele in Bosco.

Bologna is also an excellent springboard for day trips or even one-night stop-overs to Italian cities such as Modena and Ferrara. Parma, with its world-famous cheese and ham, is less than an hour away, as is the coastal resort of Rimini. Ferraris are made just up the road at Maranello and raced on the grand-prix circuit at Imola just south of Bologna, while the hills southwest of Bologna offer spa towns, trekking and winter skiing, all within easy reach by both public and private transport.

Such is the embarrassment of choice in the city that you may wish to organize your visit into themes, such as art, food, technology, or simply shopping.

Churches, art and architecture

Be daunted by the basilica of San Petronio (p32), awestruck by the delicate interwoven churches of Santo Stefano (p66). See the abundance of sculptures and fresoces by Bolognese and Renaissance masters in San Martino (p59), San Domenico (p69), San Giacomo Maggiore (p52) and Giovanni in Monte (p68). Discover the exquisite secrets upstairs in the Chiesa della Madonna del Colombano (p83). Get an overload of Bolognese masters at the city art gallery, La Pinacoteca (p58) and the Collezioni Comunali d'Arte in the Palazzo Comunale (p36). For a trip into modernity, visit the Galleria d'Arte Moderna (p85) in the Kenzo Tange-shaped Fiera (trade fair) district and in the Museo Morandi (p36) dedicated to Bologna's answer to Cezanne. For more of the modern, check out the new Manifattura delle Arti cultural centre in the former industrial sector, home of university faculties, the Cineteca and Lumière cinemas and, from 2006, the new seat of the modern art gallery.

Food

Take a culinary tour of the city's delicatessens and restaurants. See fresh pasta being made outside Trattoria Annamaria (p139). Visit the food markets of the Quadrilatero, especially Tamburini (p198). Visit the cheese factories of Parma (p105).

Technology

Visit the Ducati museum (p88), the Ferrari museum at Maranello (p108) and the Formula One circuit at Imola (p112). Go to the university museums and relive the pioneering of Marconi and

Galvani (p55). Visit the Exhibition Centre in the Fiera district to attend one of the city's many important trade fairs, especially the Motor Show (p87).

Shopping
Shop and window-shop for Italian fashion in an array of classy, chic and costly designer boutiques around town (p196). Seek out some more experimental and hip stores offering innovative Italian takes on London grunge. You can also browse for books (p195) or buy up delicious ingredients at the city's well-stocked delicatessens (p197)

Contemporary Bologna

Innovation, liberal thought and rebellion – three characteristics linked by a common challenge to the status quo – have always characterized the spirit of Bologna and its citizens. Bologna was always a restless subject of Popes, kings and ruling dynasties and its medieval history is littered with uprisings, overthrowings and general disobedience to attempted foreign authorities. The city's university, the first of its kind in Europe, was always an engine of enlightenment and discovery, from the first principles of European law and human rights to the invention of radio. And the Bolognese rejection of Mannerism, born of an innate pragmatism, founded one of the most influential schools of classical art. These three characteristics still manifest themselves today, in a different guise, running under the surface of modern life in Bologna and connecting the city to its past.

Bologna's position at the forefront of Italian technology continues to this day. Twinned with Coventry in the UK, it seems apposite that Bologna and its environs are sometimes referred to as *la terra delle moto* – the land of motorbikes – due to the concentration of car and motorbike factories located around the city. That's about as far as the comparison can stretch, however. Apart from the significant difference in architectural beauty between Bologna and its Midlands relative, the factories in question are none other than Ducati and, nearby, Ferrari, Lamborghini and Maserati. Personally I'd rather be sent to Bologna.

Independent and specialist, these famous small- and medium-sized companies are typical of the type of business to be found in Bologna and different from the cumbersome conglomerates further north. These industries have contributed to make Bologna and its surrounds one of the most affluent regions in the country, dubbed the 'Third Italy', between the industrial triangle in the north and the underdeveloped south.

Bologna is also known for its innovation in the field of fashion, and in particular *pronta moda* or off-the-peg fashion. A quick glance in the clothes shops along via dell'Indipendenza will also reveal an experimental grunge style for young and trendy Bolognese that's akin to London and a far cry from the rigidity of Barbours, V-neck jumpers and brown brogues seemingly *de rigueur* elsewhere in Italy. It is said that many of the designs that end up on the catwalks of Milan start out as experimental ideas in Bologna. Remember, you saw it first here.

Bolognese innovation in youth fashion has translated into the city's bars, cafés and nightclubs. When it comes to concept bars and wacky decor, Bologna has a greater selection than many Italian cities, reclaiming its former industrial zones and warehouses, especially to the northwest, with some surprising results. Contrary to the profoundly conservative currents running through the country, Bologna has a renowned and well-organized gay scene – a further statement of its emancipated attitude. Funky bars and clubs are packed with Bologna's arty-camp population, mixing easily with straight revellers.

Many bars serve as stages for the city's abundant artists, combining eating and drinking with short film projections, exhibitions, performance art, music, theatre and dance spectacles. Bologna and Emilia-Romagna also have a long tradition of music: nearby Parma hosts opera productions to rank alongside those of La

Scala or Verona, and Modena is birthplace of Luciano Pavarotti. Nowadays the city is, by Italian standards, a centre for jazz, hosting many international line-ups in its clubs and providing a forum for newcomers. Rock music is alive and kicking in Bologna, too. Birthplace of Lucio Dalla and beloved of Italy's only real rocker, Vasco Rossi (born in Modena), the city is a stop on the tours of many international pop acts. In 2000 Bologna was nominated a European City of Culture and like a latter-day patriarch, the progressive city council is very active in its support of artistic initiatives. The lengths of via Zamboni, the self-professed street of art and via delle Belle Arti are plastered with posters announcing the latest events going on in the city, from raves to poetry recitals.

Many of these local artists and performers are students, following in the lofty footsteps of such alumni as Dante, Boccaccio and Petrarch, but also of the enraged and engaged students of the 20th century who took Bologna's university into the political sphere. After the end of the Second World War, and as if in rebellion against the memory of its recent fascist occupation, Bologna became the centre of Socialism in Italy. From that moment on, and particularly during Italy's dark years of terrorism in the 1970s and 1980s, the city was a mouthpiece for criticism of a centre-right government that was accused by many, such as the journalist and film director Pier Paolo Pasolini, of creeping fascism. In 1977 Bologna's 70,000-strong student population took to the streets in a revolt that was their own local version of 1968. In 1980 the city became a target and received a vendetta from neo-fascist far right terrorists in the form of a massive bomb attack on the station, which killed 80 people.

Things have changed a bit since those days of meaningful activism and anarchy. Nowadays the long hair, the graffiti and the bicycles are still there, but Bologna's seemingly eternally resting modern-day students could be accused of living the image of the artist-rebel without the belief and direction of their predecessors. Nor is the city these days considered such a bastion of protest and of the left-wing principles of philanthropy, austerity and abstention. Then again, perhaps this was always the city's alluring and ultimately workable paradox. Bologna is a land of plenty, totally devoted to epicurean pleasures, whose affluence, gluttony and famed corpulence, to say nothing of its fast cars and fashion, rather take the edge off its social conscience and belie the image of the starving student. If there are any *partigiani* (partisans) left, they are more than likely of the *prosecco* variety.

Which brings us to the city's most famous ingredient – its food. Despite other regions' claims, Bologna's cuisine is the best in Italy. Cultivated, prepared, served and consumed with great pride and sensual pleasure but minimum ritual, food and wine have been Bologna's real religion since the city's foundation. Over this time the Bolognese have invented a tongue-twisting delicatessen and oral orgy of pastas, meats, cheese and sauces, from *lasagne*, *tagliatelle* and *tortellini* to *mortadella* and *squacquerone*, to name just a few. And as they have invented them, so these dishes have passed into the region's tradition. But while today's chefs respect and vaunt their city's culinary heritage, they also perceive their vocation as a process of development, a moveable or at least evolving feast, ripe for innovation. We're not talking fusion of Japanese with Moroccan food here, but specialities of the house, with subtle and significant nuances on traditional themes. The famed spirit of innovation and experimentation is expanding the territory of the city's gastronomic traditions, discovering new Dionysian delights to satisfy both gourmet and glutton.

Bologna is easily and economically accessible from the UK: the cheapest flights to the city are from London Stansted, either with Easyjet direct to Bologna airport or with Ryanair to Forlì, 45 km to the southeast.

There is no metro yet (although plans for one have been drawn up) but the city has a very efficient bus system and, generally, your feet are all you'll need to get around the centre. The most Bolognese mode of transport in the city (and by far the most fun) is either the bicycle or the moped. Both will allow access to Bologna's back streets and hidden sights. A good-value and reasonably efficient network of public transport can take you on trips out into the hills or to the surrounding cities of Parma, Ferrara, Imola, Modena and to the sea at Rimini.

If you'd like somebody to show you around, informative walking tours take you to the some of the less-discovered corners of the city, bus tours give your legs a rest, and wine and food tasting tours are a good excuse for more copious consumption of the area's produce.

Getting there

Air

From UK and Europe Both *Easyjet* and *Ryanair* have fares starting at around £60 return, if you book early enough, from London Stansted to Bologna and Forlì airports respectively. A small discount is offered for bookings made online. There are frequent scheduled flights on *British Airways* and *Alitalia* to Bologna from London's Gatwick airport, usually costing upwards of £150 return. Bologna is also connected by direct flights to many European cities including Amsterdam, Barcelona, Brussels, Copenhagen, Frankfurt, Lyon, Lisbon, Madrid, Nice, Paris, Prague, Vienna and Zurich.

From North America From June 2005 there will be direct flights between New York and Bologna, with Alitalia, Lufthansa, United, Iberia, Delta and Air France. This is the only direct route to Bologna from the US or Canada. It is, however, relatively cheap to fly via London or another European hub, such as Frankfurt or Zurich. Other options are the routings via Milan or Rome. The cheaper end of the scale costs from $500-600 upwards off-season, rising to over $1000 in the popular summer months.

From Australia and New Zealand There are no direct flights to Bologna (or anywhere else in Italy) from either Australia or New Zealand. You will have to change at least twice. You can fly to Milan and Rome via another European or Asian (eg Singapore, Kuala Lumpur) city, from where you will have to connnect again for Bologna. Airlines that fly to European cities from Australia and New Zealand include: *Alitalia*, *British Airways*, *Lufthansa*, *Malaysian Airlines*, *Qantas*, *Singapore Airlines* and *Virgin Atlantic*. The cost low season is likely to be at least A$1,700, rising to A$2,500 during high season.

→ Airlines and agents

Alitalia, **T** 0874-5448259, www.alitalia.it
British Airways, **T** 0845-7733377, www.ba.com
Ryanair, **T** 0870-1569569, www.ryanair.com
Virgin Atlantic, **T** 01293-450150, www.fly.virgin.com
Easyjet, **T** 0905 821 0905, www.**easyjet**.com
Expedia, **T** 0870-0500808, www.expedia.com
LastMinute, www.lastminute.com
STA Travel, **T** 0870-1600599, www.sta-travel.com
Travelocity, **T** 0870-8763876, www.travelocity.com
Trailfinders, **T** 020-79371234, www.trailfinders.com

Specialist travel agents in the UK

Arlbaster & Clarke Wine Tours, **T** 01730-893344,
www.arlbasterandclarke.com.
Citalia, Marco Polo House, 3-5 Lansdowne Rd, Croydon,
T 020-8686 5533.
Fine Art Travel, 15 Savile Row, London, **T** 020-7437 8553.

Getting to and from the airports **Marconi International
Airport**, **T** 051-6479615 (0630-2330), **F** 051-6479719,
www.bologna-airport.it, is 6 km northwest of the city centre. There
are two passenger terminals. All arrivals come in to terminal A.
European and domestic departures leave from Terminal A while
inter-continental departures leave from terminal B. Recently
upgraded, the airport has facilities for changing money, a bank,
restaurant, newsagent, snack bars and various shops selling gifts,
books and souvenirs. There is a large and helpful tourist information
desk in the centre of the arrivals hall, stacked with leaflets and
serviced by English-speaking staff. All the major car hire companies
also have offices here. Business facilities have recently been installed.

The best way to the centre is by taxi from the rank outside the terminal A. The journey normally costs around €12-15, depending on traffic. Alternatively, the **Bologna Aerobus** (**T** 051-290290) also connects the airport to the city centre. It runs every 15 minutes from 0540 to 2320 and takes about 20 minutes. Tickets cost €4 and are sold on board. If you have arrived on an *Easyjet* flight, you can book your own transfer through them via www.a-t-s.net/public/easyjet.

Forlì, **T** 0543-474990, **F** 0543-474909, www.forli-airport.it, is a small and rudimentary airport that has not yet caught up with its status as a budget airline destination and gateway to Bologna, or with the associated increase in international traffic. There is a direct bus service from Forlì airport to Bologna's bus station (on piazza XX Settembre next to the train station) which is timetabled to coincide with incoming flights from London, leaving 30 minutes after each flight's arrival and waiting in case of delay. It takes around 1 hour 15 minutes and costs €10 per person – buy tickets on board. There is no direct train connection between Forlì airport and Bologna so you have to go into Forlì itself. A municipal bus (€0.80) departs from the airport every 20 minutes and takes around 15 minutes to reach the train station from where provincial trains leave for Bologna every half hour or so, taking about 40 minutes and cost around €3 each way. For the return, the direct buses from Bologna to Forlì airport depart once a day at 1230, Mon-Fri, 1520 on Sat and 1315 on Sun, again to coincide with necessary check-in times for departing international flights.

Road

Car Italy has an excellent network of *autostrade* (motorways), demonstrating amazing feats of engineering in a country that is two-thirds mountain. Bologna is linked by the A1 to Milan (2 hours), Florence (1 hour) and Rome (three hours), by the A13 to Venice and Padua and by the A14 to Rimini, Ravenna and the Adriatic coast. All motorways are tolled (eg driving from Rome to

Bologna costs approximately €15); travellers on a budget might therefore prefer the *strade statali* or *SS*, which are toll-free dual carriageways. The nominal speed limit is 130 km for motorways and 110 km/h on SS, although both are conspicuously flouted by the natives. EU nationals taking their own vehicle need an International Insurance Certificate, known as a *carta verde* (green card). For more information on this, contact **Automobile Club Italiano** (**T** 06-49981, 24hrs). Emergency breakdown (ACI), **T** 116.

Bus/coach It's an arthritis-guaranteeing ride but, for the truly budget conscious, Bologna can be reached by coach from London Victoria station in about 24 hours (£71 return, contact *Eurolines UK Ltd*, **T** 08705-143219, www.gobycoach.com). Within Italy services connect the city to both Milan and Ancona in the south. Regional coaches, ambitiously called *pullman service* go to Ferrara and Modena; there is also a bus connection to Modena direct from Bologna airport. All coaches depart and arrive from the coach station in piazza XX Settembre (**T** 051-290290, www.autostazionebo.it) just round the corner from the train station. Check timetables at the bus station on arrival, as these are subject to change.

Train

Bologna Centrale (**T** 051-6391311) is at piazza Medaglie d'Oro to the north of the city. Several car hire companies (*Avis*, *Hertz*, *Maggiore*) have offices here and other facilities include banks, bars, restaurants, newspaper stalls and a pharmacy. The heart of the city is a 15 minute walk up via dell'Indipendenza. Alternatively take bus 10, 25 or 30 (purchase a ticket from *tabacchi* (tobacconists) designated by a white 'T' in a black box outside the shops). For timetable information and bookings, contact **TrenItalia**, **T** 800-915030 (*0700-1930, from within Italy*) or visit the website www.trenitalia.com

    Bologna is a major junction on Italy's railway network, making it very accessible to other Italian cities and European destinations further afield. Italy's own *Eurostar* currently links Bologna to Milan (2 hours), Florence (1 hour), Rome (3 hours) and Naples (5 hours) while the *Eurocity* connects passengers with more than 40 other European destinations including Paris, Basel and Brussels. The Italian state railway, recently rebranded *TrenItalia*, is more efficient than mythology would have it. It is also one of the most economical in Europe, fares in both directions being charged by the kilometre. Once bought, a ticket is not valid until it has been stamped (before boarding) in one of the yellow machines on the platform. There are five types of train, divided according to speed and the frequency with which they stop. *Diretto*, *Inter-regionale* and *Espresso* all stop frequently and only require a standard ticket whereas supplements are usually required on the faster *Intercity* and *Eurostar* services.

Getting around

Central Bologna is easily covered on foot. It takes just under an hour to walk from one side of the Centro Storico to the other.

Bicycle and moped

Bologna's bikes are the honest, old-fashioned, sit-up-and-beg type, robust enough to withstand the cobbles. Expect to be looked at quizzically if you ask for a helmet; such things have not yet been absorbed into the Italian image. Impassable, narrow streets make Bolognese cyclists relatively immune to fast traffic, however, so you should be OK. For bike hire, see p216.

Bus

The centre and suburbs are covered by an efficient network of orange buses run by the **ATC** (*Trasporti Pubblici Bologna*, **T** 051-290290, www.atc.bo.it). Information on services can be found in the train and coach station in piazza XX Settembre as well as at their city office on via Marconi. A simple ticket costs €1 and lasts an hour from the time you validate it in the machine upon boarding. Within this time you can use the same ticket on as many buses and for as many journeys as you wish. Alternatively, and better value, the City Pass is valid for up to seven journeys (of up to one hour each) across multiple days and costs €6.50. There is also a *giornaliero* (day ticket) which costs €3 and lasts 24 hours from validation. All bus tickets can be purchased at *tabacchi* (tobacconists/newsagents – marked with a 'T' outside), bars and newspaper kiosks. For information, see the website or call **T** 051-290290, 0700-2000. *Controllori* intermittently patrol the buses in blue uniforms or sometimes plain clothes. The penalty for not having a valid ticket is around €50, payable on the spot.

Buses leave the coach station in piazza XX Settembre every hour for Ferrara and take 45 minutes. They leave every 15 minutes for Imola and take an hour. There are also regular buses to Parma. Tickets to all these cost in the region of €12-20 return.

Car
Unless you have arrived by car, driving in the city is to be avoided. The centre is compact and easily covered on foot or with public transport. Parking is also very difficult. The Centro Storico is officially closed to private vehicles every day from 0700-2000 although this restriction does not apply to guests staying in the centre provided that they register with the police on arrival. Your hotel should be able to do this for you. Many hotels also have private parking for guests for which a supplement is usually charged. The city does operate a park and ride scheme, details of which are available from the *ATC* office (see p25).

Taxi
Taxis in Italy are generally expensive as drivers will find any excuse to justify various add-ons. If booked by phone you will be charged for the journey to pick you up. Although technically possible, do not try to hail a taxi in the street. You might as well be waving to someone

on the other side. It's best to queue up at the ranks in piazza Maggiore or outside the train station, or better still, think ahead and book by phone via the city's taxi co-operative on **T** 051-372727.

Train
Trains run frequently from Bologna to Ferrara, Modena and Imola, all taking around half an hour. Ravenna is about 40 minutes by direct train, as is Rimini. Parma is about 45 minutes. There are also frequent trains from Ravenna to the coast. Tickets to all these destinations cost in the region of €8-12 single.

Tours

The tourist office has a full list of the companies and organizations that run guided tours of Bologna. Some of these are special-interest tours and all offer the service in at least five languages. There are currently no bus tours of the city.

Le Guide d'Arte, via del Monte 5, **T** 051-2750254, www.guidedarte.com, specializes in Bologna's art history.

GAIA, piassa Roosevelt 4, **T** 051-2960005, www.guidebologna.com, offers general interest tours.

Strada dei Vini e dei Sapori T 0542-25413, www.stradavinni esapori.it Food and wine-tasting tours into the villages and vineyards in the Apennine hills around Imola.

Walking tours

Well-paced, informative multi-lingual walking tours of the city are provided by **Discover Bologna/Scopri Bologna**, **T** 051-246541, 1030 on Wednesdays, Saturday and Sundays from the *IAT* (Ufficio Informazioni e Accoglienza Turistica), piazza Maggiore 1; also try

Prima Classe (**T** 0347-8944094), 1100 from the Fontana Nettuno on Sundays. Both cost €13 per person. One-on-one guides arranged through **Associazione Guida d'Arte**, **T** 051-4210809, cost around €60 for three hours.

Tourist information

Bologna Turismo, under Palazzo Podesta, piazza Maggiore 1, **T** 051-246541, www.bolognaturismo.info, *daily 0900-1900*. The office provides more free maps and leaflets than you could possibly need. Within the same building is the *Emporio della Cultura* – selling a host of books, souvenirs and tickets for events, and the *CST* (Hotel Reservation Centre). There are also offices at the rail station and airport, offering equally abundant free information.

Emilia Romagna Turismo, via Aldo Moro 10, **F** 051-284122, www.emiliaromagnaturismo.it The website provides information on cities, towns and villages throughout Emilia Romagna, with suggested itineraries and details of where to stay, where to eat, prices and festivals as well as useful links and contact details.

Around Bologna
Ferrara Castello Estense, T 0532-209370; **Ravenna**   via Salara 8/12, **T** 0544 482670, turismorav@provincia.ra.it; **Modena**   piazza Grande 17, **T** 059-206660, iatmo@comune.modena.it, *Mon-Fri 0930-1230, 1530-1830. Sat 0930-1230*; **Parma** via Melloni 1B, **T** 0521-218889, www.turismo.commune.parma.it; **Rimini** piazzale F Fellini 3, **T** 0541-56902, iat2@iper.net *0900-1200, 1500-1900*.

Centre: piazza Maggiore and around 31

The two conjoining squares of piazza Maggiore and piazza Nettuno are the social hub of the city.

Northeast: the university quarter 47

A lively and bohemian atmosphere comprising 17th- and 18th-century palazzos, porticoed streets and intriguing alleys.

Southeast: Santo Stefano and around 63

Bologna's most picturesque, stately and tranquil district, with a fascinating piazza at its heart.

Southwest: around via del Pratello 76

From the elegant catwalk of via d'Azeglio, to boozy uproarious *osterie*.

Northwest: around via Galliera 80

Modern concrete dotted with a few old streets and a watery, industrial underground history.

Exhibition centre and around 86

Shiny towers, trade fairs and modern art.

Hills to the south 89

The foothills of the Apennines begin just outside the city walls with villas, parks and the 666 arches of the Portico di San Luca.

Centre: piazza Maggiore and around

The space of piazza Maggiore exerts an almost magnetic pull on visitors and locals alike so that you will inevitably start or end up here. Standing in the middle of the entirely pedestrianized piazza you feel you could be in the central courtyard of a great castle, enclosed and protected by towers: the tall, thick and crenellated masses of the **Palazzo Comunale** *and* **Palazzo Podesta** *and the forbidding weight of the* **Basilica di San Petronio**, *whose faceless façade makes it more like a fortification than a place of worship. This is the site of the ancient Roman forum and the city's most emblematic buildings. Until the 19th century, the square was the city's main market place and it still teems with life, from wandering locals on their passeggiata to swarms of visiting school children. A perfect meeting place, the piazza also offers a wonderful shop window onto Italian life. Sit back and observe the Italians as they do what they do best: hanging around for no discernible reason but looking so cool and well-groomed for it not to matter. Apart from this daily social theatre, the piazza serves as Bologna's answer to Covent Garden and there is usually some freelance art show. A forum for coronations and executions in Roman times, the piazza now stages anything from puppet shows to the ubiquitous international Peruvian panpipe band.*

▸▸ *See Sleeping p117, Eating and drinking p134, Bars and clubs p167*

 Sights

Fontana del Nettuno
Map 4, D3, p256

Bologna's bronze statue of the Roman God of the Sea might as well have been conceived as a statue to the God of Photography, so much has it become a symbol of the city and a favourite backdrop for posing visitors who adorn the *putti* (chubby cherubs) and mermaids at his feet. Completed between 1563 and 1566 and known affectionately as *il Gigante* due to its size, the statue is the work of the Flemish sculptor Jean de Boulogne (known in Italian as Giambologna) and is based on a design by Tommaso Laureti. The statue was commissioned by bishop Pier Donato Cesi as part of an urban beautification programme requested by the then Pope Pio IV and aimed at making papal Bologna the second city in Italy after Rome. On the side of the Palazzo Comunale is another fountain, referred to as *la fontana vecchia* (old fountain), older than the Neptune fountain but also designed by Tommaso Laureti.

★ Basilica di San Petronio
piazza Maggiore, **T** 051-225442. *0730-1300, 1430-1830 in winter, until 1930 in summer. Free. Map 4, E3, p256*

It seems highly unlikely that the vast expense involved in constructing Bologna's basilica to her patron saint would ever be tolerated by democracies today. The building of San Petronio cost both huge amounts of money and numerous lives, and required the demolition of many churches and houses. As the façade and half-arches down the western exterior tell, the ambition was never fully realized. Funded by public money, the basilica, which is a civic temple not a cathedral, was conceived by the elected city council as a monument of opposition to the Papacy in Rome and was originally intended to be larger than St Peter's. The Papacy grew fearful of this ambition and diverted money and land to the construction of the Archiginnasio and founding of the university. The models in the

! Legend has it that prior to commencing work on the design of the Fontana del Nettuno, and preoccupied with the ample nudity of the pagan God, Giambologna sought an approval from the Pope. "For Bologna it's ok" came the answer, an early confirmation of the city's fame in Italy as a centre for more liberal attitudes and emancipated thinking.

church **museum** in the annex (**T** 051-223256, *1000-1200 except Tue and Thu, free*) show that what is currently standing is only one-fifth of a project that foresaw a longer nave, transept and a 150-m high dome. That said, at 132 m in length, it is still one of the largest churches in Christendom. Designed in a late Gothic style by the architect Antonio di Vicenzo, the first stone was laid in 1390 and the current state reached only after several centuries of labour. Aside from the lower arches down its side which were constructed from the stone of demolished houses, the pale, main bulk of the church is rather plain and unspectacular, emphasizing the deceit that would have been the façade had it been completed. Its base is embellished with stripes of red Veronese marble and white Istrian stone whereas the charcoal-coloured top two-thirds of the façade remain bare, giving the basilica a blunt aspect, as ugly as it is intriguing.

The vast interior, too, seems empty and dour, with amplified supplications echoing around like platform announcements. That said, God is in the details and, on closer inspection, the basilica does have many redeeming features. The first of these are the unfinished figures in the half-moon above the central portal. Begun in 1425 by the Renaissance master Jacopo della Quercia, they depict the Madonna and Child, St Petronius and St Ambrosius and, either side of the door, stories from the Old Testament. Just above the door there used also to be a rare bronze figurine of Pope Julius II made by Michelangelo in 1508. In an act of Ghibelline anti-papal disrespect the figurine was plundered and melted down into ammunition for the wars between the Bentivoglio and Este dynasties. Meanwhile, also by della Quercia are the bas-reliefs on the nave pillars depicting stories from both the Old and New Testaments.

The basilica contains 22 side chapels with paintings, sculptures, glasswork, faience and marquetry by many Bolognese hands. Perhaps the most exquisite of these is the Cappella Bolognini, financed by the Bolognini family's silk empire, with its frescoes by Giovanni de Modena depicting the *Journey of the Three Kings*, *Paradise* and, most spectacularly, *Hell*.

The intact skull of St Petronius has been preserved in the second left-hand chapel, where there are also frescoes, depicting the saint's life. The astronomical clock created in 1655 by Gian Domenico Cassini and Domenico Guglielmi illustrates the links between the basilica and the city as a centre of exploration and discovery. As a direct result of their studies of Galileo's theories at the city's university, the two men conceived of this outsize sundial, whose length, precisely 67.72 m, equals 1/600,000th of the earth's circumference. At noon the sunlight entering by means of a hole in the ceiling hits this line and throughout the year travels from one end to the other, enabling measurement of the exact date of the summer and winter solstices. The marble slabs along the line indicate the days and months and also the signs of the zodiac. It was this line which led to the discovery of the anomalies in the Julian calendar (in 1532 the spring equinox arrived too early) and ultimately to the invention of leap years and the reform of the calendar by Pope Gregory XII, after whom the modern Gregorian calendar is named.

● *If you want refreshment and a rest for your neck after visiting the Basilica, avoid the crowds in the cafés on piazza Maggiore, duck into via Clavature and enjoy a cappuccino at Rosa Rose (see p168).*

Palazzo Comunale

piazza Maggiore 6, **T** 051-201111. *Tue-Sat 0930-1830, Sun 1000-1830, closed Mon. Entry to galleries €4; 15-18-year-olds €2; under-15s free.   Map 4, C2-D3, p256*

It is hard to believe that the fortress-like citadel that occupies the entire west flank of piazza Maggiore, encompassing a total of 15,000 sq m, is merely the city's town hall. Built in 1287, it is more like a small city within a city. Commissioned by Cardinal Anglic de Grimoard in 1336 to encircle the complex, the considerable defences were conceived as a show of strength by the Papacy and to defend it from warring Ghibellines. The building is sometimes also referred to as the Palazzo d'Accursio after the original owner of the real estate.

Other than for its sheer grandiosity, the building is notable for a number of outstanding features. The clocktower, Bologna's answer to Big Ben, was built in 1773 by Rinaldo Gandolfi. The famous terracotta *Madonna and Child* which adorns the façade was completed in 1478 by a sculptor from Puglia, Niccolo dell'Arca. The large classical groundfloor window is the design of Galeazzo Alessi (no relation to the homewares designer) below which are two marble eagles, the left of which is attributed to Michelangelo. On the wall below is a plaque which sets out the decreed standards of measurement in medieval times (the foot, the double arm and the perch) to avoid cheating and arguments between traders. Perhaps the most striking feature is the huge finger-wagging statue of Bologna-born Pope Gregory XIII (he of the calendar) produced by Menganti between 1576 and 1580. In contrast to many of Bologna's other main buildings, which are robust in their symbolic defiance of papal control, this statue, commissioned at a time when Bologna was controlled from Rome, was by its size designed to leave the citizens in no doubt as to who was boss. Ironically, by the time of the Napoleonic invasions, the Bolognese had become so proud of this symbol of their city, they dressed it up as St Petronius to save it from destruction by the French Emperor's anti-papal army.

The ground floor of the Palazzo was once used as a market and warehouse for grain. The magnificent first floor hall is reached via a beautiful passage with a sloping wooden causeway, so designed by Bramante for easy access by noblemen on horseback or in sedan chairs. At the top of these stairs is the Sala di Ercole ('Hercules' room', after the terracotta statue of the hero there by Lombardi). This room is decorated in beautiful frescoes, among which Tibaldi's *Vigiliance*, Ludovico Carracci's *Phaeton's Fall*, the *Madonna* by Lippo di Dalmasio and the *Madonna and the Earthquake* by Francesco Francia are the most famous. The inside courtyard contains interesting rooms, many of which are open to visitors. The most important of these is probably the **Sala Farnese**, home of the **Collezioni Comunali d'Arte**, the city public art collection, which includes paintings and frescoes by many masters of the Bolognese school such as Signorelli, the Caracci brothers and Jacopo di Paolo, and works by Tintoretto. Nowadays, rooms of the Palazzo Comunale are used for a variety of events from receptions and functions to product launches, musical performances, temporary art exhibitions and even mild raves; they can be visited by the public at other times.

Museo Morandi

Palazzo Communale, piazza Maggiore 6, **T** 051-203646/203629. *1000-1800, Tue-Sun. Closed Mon. €4. Map 4, D2, p256*

Adjacent to the Sala Farnese within the Palazzo Comunale complex, this recently established museum has the largest collection (over 200 works) of Giorgio Morandi, Bologna's most famous contemporary artist (see p37). Morandi's gentle simplicity, mellow colours and his more mundane subject matter may provide a refreshing change from the classical art and religious imagery prevalent in the city. The museum also contains a reconstruction of the artist's studio at via Fondazza 36, providing an insight into his work and methods.

Palazzo Podesta and Palazzo Re Enzo

piazza Maggiore. *Closed to public except during exhibitions. Map 4, C3-D3, p256*

The castle-like construction in the centre of piazza Maggiore in fact combines two buildings, the Palazzo Podesta and the Palazzo Re Enzo. Before becoming the governor's residence, the Palazzo Podesta was originally designed in the early 13th century to house the city's law court. Of the original structure only the Arengo tower, built in 1212, remains. The belfry with its *campanazzo*

▶ **Giorgio Morandi (1890-1964)**

Morandi was born in Bologna and spent most of his life painting there or in the village of Vergato, 40 km from the city. His landscapes have been compared to the work of Cezanne for the recurring presence of similarly angular shapes and soft hues. Painting during a period of immense social upheaval, technological innovation and artistic explosion, he was initially drawn towards the work of the Futurists and Cubists. But ultimately he found his peace in more metaphysical painting, aligning himself with the artists Carra and De Chirico. He became the artist of simple everyday things: vases, fruit, windows, discovering them as if for the first time, revealing their hidden depths, and imbuing them with an existential significance. He once said, "Everything is a mystery, ourselves and the most simple, most infinitesimal of things."

(literally 'bloody great bell' – it weighs 4700kg) was added in 1453. The building's current form was the work of Giovanni II of the ruling Bentivoglio dynasty, who took a keen interest in embellishing the city and commissioned the architect Aristotele Fioravanti to renovate and redesign it. Particularly notable are the terracotta statues by Alfonso Lombardi on the pillars that support the tower, representing the city's patron saints, and the bas-reliefs of different animals that decorate the columns of the portico.

● *If you stand at the junction of the four passages at the foot of the belfry under the Palazzo Podesta, facing the wall and whisper, anyone standing diametrically opposite and facing the wall can hear what you are saying (traffic permitting). It is said that cheating lovers used to meet here to exchange sweet-nothings without fear of being discovered.*

Built in 1244, as an extra wing of the Palazzo del Podesta for civic functions the **Palazzo Re Enzo** takes its name from the man who was its prisoner for 22 years. Enzo, the blonde young king of Sardinia, was the illegitimate son of Frederick the Great, ruler of the occupying imperial army in the early 13th century. In 1249 the papal Guelph forces won a historic victory over Frederick at the battle of nearby Fossalta and took his son prisoner. He was detained in this building until his untimely death there in 1271. The building became known as Enzo's *dorata prigione* (golden prison) on account of the luxury in which he was kept, complete with cooks, maids and courtiers to keep him entertained. The palazzo was restored at the beginning of the 20th century, salvaging the beautiful wooden vaulted staircase that leads up to various assembly rooms now used for exhibitions and meetings.

● *At the time when the main piazza was also used for executions, the executioner's wife, Lazzarina, kept flower pots next to the bodies of the hanged criminals displayed on the iron balustrade of the Palazzo Podesta. The expression "to end up in Lazzarina's garden" (the equivalent of "sleeping with the fishes") entered popular local parlance, although it has since fallen into disuse.*

Palazzo dei Notai
piazza Maggiore. *Mon and Wed 0900-1300, Tue, Thu and Fri 1500-1900. Map 4, D3, p256*

Nestled between the basilica and the town hall is the Hall of the Notaries. With its modest proportions and Gothic windows with their triforas and marble columns, it is more ornate and pleasing to the eye than the monsters which sandwich it. The oldest part of the building opposite the town hall dates back to the 13th century while the rest was added in the late 15th century. The building was the seat of the city Guild of Notaries and place of study for some of the legal scholars at Bologna's university who pioneered many of the basic principles of European law.

▶ Of Guelphs and Ghibellines

The conflict between the Guelphs and the Ghibellines was a major feature of 13th-century Italy. Guelphs were followers of the Pope, while Ghibellines supported the Emperor, Frederick the Great. Alliances for each side divided the country's many controlling family dynasties. In Bologna the two families to whom the conflicting factions allied themselves were, on one side, the Geremei, who were Guelphs and, on the other, the Lambertazzi family, who were Ghibellines.

Following their victory at the battle of Fossalta in 1249, the Guelphs took control of the city and submitted it to the control of Pope Nicholas III, who from 1278 ruled the city by proxy from Rome. However, despite this yoke, Bologna was always allowed to enjoy relative autonomy for fear of further insurrection.

Bologna's buildings tell of a history of oscillation between papal and imperial forces. They were usually conceived as statements of the preeminence of one power over the other and were often altered by a new incumbent in deliberate architectural snubs.

Perhaps the most famous example of the Guelph-Ghibelline conflict, however, lies further north in Verona, where, at the same time as the battle of Fossalta, two young lovers were trying to transcend their families' different allegiances. Their names, of course, were Romeo and Juliet.

Palazzo dei Banchi
piazza Maggiore. *Closed to the public.* Map 4, D4, p256

Completing the enclosure of the square on its eastern side, the Bankers' House (1412) is so named after the bankers and money lenders who use to have *banchi* ('benches' or stalls) under its arcades (indeed this is the origin of our word 'bank'). Originally a row of jumbled buildings, they were brought together in the 16th century by the architect Vignola to create the present harmonious façade that is oddly classical compared to many of Bologna's old buildings. It is possible that the façade also served to hide from the eyes of the medieval nobles the group of narrow streets immediately behind the Palazzo, known as the Quadrilatero. These were populated at the time by the lower classes and small-time tradesmen. The majestic row of arcades underneath the façade is known as *il Pavaglione*. In the days when the piazza was used as a weekly market, this area was where the cocoons of the *pava* (silkworm) were sold under a large protective marquee or pavilion.

★ Il Quadrilatero and il Mercato di Mezzo
Map 4, D4-D5, p256

Il Quadrilatero is the name given to the grid of narrow streets hidden behind the east of piazza Maggiore. These streets were home to the small businessmen of medieval Bologna and each street still bears the name of the powerful associations of artisans and merchants it was known for: *orefici* (jewellers), *clavature* (locksmiths), *pescherie* (fishmongers), *drapperie* (textile merchants). The grid, itself part of the original Roman settlement, used to extend further north but the roads were flattened to make way for via Rizzoli and piazza Ravegnana in line with the 19th-century fashion for boulevards. Today these are still among Bologna's liveliest market streets. By day they are full of the smells, colours and cries of butchers, grocers and the fresh local produce that makes the cuisine of this city so rich. By night they become the stage for Bologna's beautiful youth as they strut in and out of the many bars that have become some of the city's trendiest early evening nightspots.

Santuario di Santa Maria della Vita
via Clavature 10, **T** 051-236245. *0700-1800*. *Map 4, D4, p256*

You could be forgiven for missing this tiny church amid the bustle of the market streets of the Quadrilatero and its presence in such a hive of trade seems incongruous. Originally built in the late 14th century to house the ill and impoverished folk of this quarter, the church grew a dome and became home to one of the unrivalled works of beauty in Bologna's treasure chest of fine art: the dramatic *Three Marys Lament over the Dead Christ*, by the sculptor Niccolò dell'Arca. Mary's desperation was once described by the poet Gabriele d'Annunzio as "a petrified scream". The next door oratory, also home to the Museo della Sanita, houses a famous group of 14 similarly expressive terracotta statues by Alfonso Lombardi called *Death of the Virgin*. These sculptures, realistic in their portrayal of human suffering, were in their time considered unworthy compared to the fashion for more idealized renderings of the narrative.

★ Palazzo dell'Archiginnasio
Piazza Galvani 1, via dell'Archiginnasio. *Mon-Fri 0900-1800, Sat 0900-1330*. *Map 4, F4, p253*

This rose-coloured building on the eastern flank of piazza Galvani, with its beautiful 139 m-long portico, was the seat of Bologna's university from 1563 until 1803 when it was transferred to via Zamboni. The idea, conceived by a professor of law named Pier Donato Cesi, was to bring together under one roof the various faculties of the university, which had, since the 11th century, cropped up in a disordered way around the city.

The beautiful interior courtyard with its double loggia is also noted for the 7000 or so heraldic shields emblazoned under the arches. These shields replaced tower-building as the fashion by which noblemen, eminent professors, students and rich people could immortalize their families. Such was the rush for wall space that shields were often disfigured by competing families, leading to a law being passed to prevent such profanation.

The site is divided into two halves representing two basic distinctions in the realm of study that were made by the university, the southern half for Law and the northern half for students of the Arts (including mathematics and natural sciences). Under the loggia in the main courtyard is the Santa Maria dei Bulgari chapel which has some remnants of frescoes by Bartolomeo Ceso.

Within the Archiginnasio complex lies the **Teatro Anatomico** (*Mon-Sat 0900-1300, Mon-Fri 1300-1830*), the beautiful dissection theatre made entirely out of wood and resembling a law court with delicately *écorché* wood statues of skinned torsos by Giannotti. Built in 1637 it is a replica of the original 1595 room where the importance of human dissection to medicine was first demonstrated, often to mass audiences. Dissections were only carried out in the winter months as Zanussi had not yet invented the fridge.

The Archiginnasio also houses the **Biblioteca Comunale** (municipal library), located here since 1838 and containing over 700,000 books and a collection of rare manuscripts that make it one of the most important libraries in Italy. The whole building suffered badly in a bombing raid in January 1944 but was skillfully restored to its current state.

Museo Civico Archeologico

via dell'Archiginnasio 2, **T** 051-2757211. *Tue-Sat 0900-1830, Sun 1000-1830, Closed Mon. €4, concessions €2, under-14s free . Map 4, E4, p256*

This 14th-century building, itself a section of the Pavaglione, was formerly the Ospedale di Santa Maria della Morte, a hospital for the terminally ill and for criminals sentenced to death. In the 16th century it underwent refurbishment before, in 1881, becoming the home of the museum of municipal archaeology. Local archaeology might be a bit of a niche interest to the average visitor and the museum does have a rather stuffy atmosphere. That said, there is a rich collection of Egyptian artefacts and bas-reliefs (second in Italy only to the collection in Turin), various Greek and Roman antiquities, including a bust of Emperor Nero, and an important collection of relics from the Etruscan civilization that made Bologna (or Felsina as they named it) the capital of northern Etruria and one of the most important economic centres from around the fifth century BC.

Metropolitana di San Pietro
Via dell'Indipendenza 7, **T** 051-222112. *0730-1200, 1600-1830 daily. Free. Map 4, B4, p256*

Bologna's squat cathedral sits flush with one of the city's busiest streets like a plump bishop. As a result it feels rather shut in and, unlike its publicly funded rival, San Petronio, does not benefit from any surrounding space which would make it possible really to admire its façade or which might enable it to dominate or inspire awe in humble and fearful citizens in the way it was intended. That said, the two 13th-century lions in Veronese marble by Mastro Ventura that guard its entrance are magnificent and the vast interior conceals a number of beautiful terracotta figures and frescoes by hands of the Bolognese school, most notably the *Annunciation* by Ludovico Carracci in the sacristy. The 12th-century belfry by Mastro Alberto is also considered a masterpiece. Otherwise the overall building is a composite of ruins and refurbishments made to the original ninth-century Holy Roman church site that has suffered fires and earthquakes down the ages. Only a beautiful spiral column inside, supported by the statue of a crossed legged man, remains from its former elegance. Every year in May the image of Bolognese saint *la Madonna di San Luca* is brought down here from her sanctuary on the hill (see Festivals, p191).

● *Turning out of the church and left into via Altabella you find the remains of an arch known as the porta dei laureati (gate of the graduates) through which new graduates once passed.*

Chiesa e Convento di San Salvatore
via Volto Santo 1, **T** 051-222852. *0730-1200, 1500-1900.*
Map 4, D1, p256

Constructed in the 17th century, this church is unusual in Bologna for its single nave and the echoes of Roman classicism in both the exterior and interior. Many important pictures are to be found in the various chapels inside, most notably perhaps the *Crowning of the Virgin* by Vitale da Bologna. The figure of Thomas Becket, one of the university's famous alumni, appears in the *Presentation of the Virgin and of St Thomas of Canterbury* by Girolamo da Treviso. This church also houses the tomb of *Il Guercino*, Giovani Francesco Barbieri, one of the greatest Italian painters of the 17th century. The associated 16th-century Augustine convent with its three cloisters of double loggias and delicate columns is an impressive monument for its deceptive size alone.

Piazza Roosevelt
Map 4, C1-D2, p256

As its name suggests this square to the west of piazza Maggiore belongs to a more recent period in Bologna's history and was in fact built on the ruins that ensued from the Allied bombardments in 1943. Unattributed holes from shrapnel are still visible on the walls opposite the Palazzo Comunale.

Palazzo Caprara
via IV Novembre 24. *Map 4, C-D1, p256*

Not many police forces nowadays can boast an HQ as beautiful as this early 17th-century nobleman's palace, commissioned by Carlo Caprara, Master of the Horse of the Emperor. Caprara had inflated ideas of the residence that would best reflect his station in life but, unfortunately, he couldn't keep up repayments on the palace and had to sell. Subsequent occupants gradually relieved the palace of its art heritage so that, now, only the façade hints at its former splendour. Napoleon stayed at Palazzo Caprara during his brief sojourn in Bologna at the end of the 18th century.

Palazzo Marescalchi
via IV Novembre 5. *Map 4, D1-2, p256*

Another of Bologna's majestic 17th-century noble houses, this palazzo is noted for its more than usually intricate exterior embellishments. Also impressive is the art on display in its drawing room, most notably the *Allegory of Air and Fire* by Guido Reni and a host of other decorations by other Bolognese hands.

★ Biblioteca Multimediale Sala Borsa
Piazza Nettuno 3, **T** 051-204400. *Map 4, C3, p256*

Alongside the Palazzo Comunale and near the old city mint in via della Zecca (road of the mint) is Bologna's former stock exchange. This is Bologna's only art-deco building, complete with stained-glass roof and cast-iron columns. It was commissioned in 1883 as a stock exchange but fell into disuse in 1903 due to lack of trade. In 1989 remains of the Roman forum were uncovered beneath the floor. These are visible through a glass floor and can now occasionally be visited on pre-arranged guided tours (**T** 051-522401; €6, under-12s free; *booking essential*).

The Ex-Sala Borsa is now the pride of Bologna's contemporary urban development plans – a multimedia exhibition hall and library, boasting tens of networked computers containing all sorts of documentation on contemporary culture and Bologna's history. The library is particularly well-equipped for children.

Associazione Amici delle Acque e dei Sotterranei di Bologna

Viale Pietramellara 11, **T** 051 522401, www.amicidelleacque.com
Booking essential. Map 2, D5, p252

As hinted elsewhere in this guide, Bologna has a hidden past as a city of underground passages and waterways. These can now be explored, following their recent opening to the public and the formation of a dedicated asssociation for their preservation. There are five locations to visit:

The **Bagni di Mario**, via Bagni de Mario 8/10, was built in the 16th century on the site of a natural reservoir to feed the Fontana Nettuno. It was designed by Tommaso Laurenti to a commission from Pope Pio IV.

The **Aposa**, on piazza Minghetti, was the main single irrigation channel on which the city was first founded and which was covered over for reasons of hygiene.

The **Bova** was the old port. It marked the confluence of the Canale Cavaticcio and the Canale delle Moline and the start of the Canale Navile. The port once stood outside the city walls until it was transferred inside to via Don Minzoni in 1550.

Il **Cavaticcio** was a tributary of the Canale Navile and wasn't used for productive purposes until 1995, when the hydroelectric powerstation was built.

The **Remonda** was an old spring that used to provide water for the hospitals nearby, until it was connected to the Bagni dei Mario to provide water for the fountain in the piazza above.

!
•
For details of the canals that provided essential water, power and transportation for the medieval city, see p60.

Northeast: the university quarter

*This area is characterized by shadowy porticoed streets that conceal buzzing and experimental cafés, bars, canteens by day and fine restaurants and underground clubs by night, mostly designed to suit the student pocket. Heralded by the city's famous **Due Torri** (two towers) at its head, the main artery of university life is **via Zamboni**, along which are the university's faculty buildings and the bars in which the students spend their time 'revising'. Halfway along, **piazza Verdi** is the veritable heart of studentland, and also theatreland, while at the other end, at the junction with via delle Belle Arti, is the famous **Pinacoteca** art museum.*

*Heading instead due north from via Rizzoli, the atmosphere changes from the mystery of the winding medina-like alleys of the old **ghetto Ebraico** (Jewish ghetto), to the refined air of the boutiques of **via Oberdan** and beyond them the less-visited working-class back streets that conceal Bologna's ancient system of waterways on **via delle Moline** and **via Piella**. To the west, just off the via dell' Indipendenza, is the city's cathedral of **San Pietro** while further north the streets open out into **piazza VIII Agosto**, stage of the city's bustling weekend market. Returning to the two towers and heading directly east the more sedate and tranquil **via San Vitale** is home to old noble residences and an abundance of antique and craft shops.*

▶▶ *See Sleeping p119, Eating and drinking p136, Bars and clubs p169*

◉ Sights

★ La Torre degli Asinelli and La Torre Garisenda
La Torre degli Asinelli. *0900-1800 in summer, until 1700 in winter.* €3. *Map 4, C5, p256*

Known colloquially as *Le Due Torri*, Bologna's twin towers have become the city's most immediately recognizable icon, its Leaning Tower of Pisa. Yet despite their apparent solitude on the city's

… the city… [is] further marked in the traveller's remembrance by the two brick leaning towers (sufficiently unsightly in themselves, it must be acknowledged), inclining cross-wise as if they were bowing stiffly to each other, a most extraordinary termination to the perspective of some of the narrow streets.

Charles Dickens, Pictures from Italy *(1866)*

skyline there used to be many more towers. In the 12th and 13th centuries any self-respecting Bolognese noble family had a tower and so intense was this practice of keeping up with the Joneses, or not wanting to be vertically challenged by your neighbour that, at the peak of their construction, Bologna's cityscape boasted over one hundred towers. In this time the city was known affectionately as *la turrita* (the towered one) and must have looked, as observed by the English traveller, H V Morton, "like a bed of asparagus." It was in the urban regeneration program of 1889 that the engineer Giuseppe Ceri campaigned vociferously for Bologna's "old and useless" towers to be pulled down. The aberration was approved, proving that the 20th century did not have a monopoly on bad architectural taste, and the *Due Torri* are two of only a few towers of any significant height that survive. These early skyscrapers served as watch-towers to warn against an attack on the city and as a place of refuge should such an attack penetrate the walls. In the 14th century they also had a brief role as a prison. Nowadays, beyond being a tourist attraction, the *Due Torri* serve as reception masts, a use of which Marconi, the Bolognese inventor of radio, would surely have approved.

At a height of nearly 98 m, **La Torre degli Asinelli** is the taller of the two, commissioned in the early 12th century by the powerful Asinelli family from which it takes its name. There are 498 sturdy oak steps leading to the top, twisting like an Escher fantasy around the inside wall, which is otherwise hollow, and providing for many cosy trysts on the way up and down. Smog permitting, the reward at the top is a stunning view over the city's rooftops to Bologna's guardian angel, the Basilica di San Luca to the southwest. On a clear day you can see as far as the Adriatic to the east and the Alps to the north.

Built almost simultaneously, the leaning **Torre Garisenda** (*closed to the public*), was originally much higher than its current 47.5 m. It started to lurch through subsidence in the mid 1300s and was truncated from its original 77 m for fear that it might topple.

One urban myth has it that the tower was built at an angle as an alternative in the tower-vanity stakes. Romantic legend suggests that one of the young Garisenda noblemen was in love with a fair Asinelli maiden and asked that the tower be built like this so that he could touch his beloved's hair. Taking a leaf out of his own book, the hedonistic French poet Theophile Gauthier, likened the two towers to two mates stumbling home and leaning on each other, drunk.

● *At the foot of the Garisenda tower you can see an inscription quoting the reference made to the tower in Canto XXXI of the Inferno of Dante's Divina Commedia, where the poet uses it as a simile for the looming giant, Antaeus.*

Chiesa di San Bartolomeo
piazza di Porta Ravegnana. 0700-1300, 1500-1630.
Map 4, D6, p256

Just behind the two towers this small church, whose reconstruction in the 16th century was left unfinished, contains some lovely frescoes, particularly the *San Carlo al sepolcro di Varallo* by Ludovico Carracci in the second right-hand chapel and Guido Reni's *Vergine col Putto* in the eighth.

Ghetto Ebraico
Map 4, B5-6, p256

Just behind the contemporary via Rizzoli the atmosphere changes and the alleyways take on a mysterious, secretive and labyrinthine aspect more resonant of an Arabian medina. Hemmed in by via Goito and full of evocatively named streets such as via dell'Inferno (Hell Street) this was formerly Bologna's Jewish ghetto. Although it is thought that the Jewish community was allowed to contribute much to Bologna's cultural beginnings in the 12th century, in the 1500s they were, as in many cities, ghettoized, and forced to live in this confined area in constant fear of persecution. To guard against attack they built spy-holes into their doors, which are still visible, for example at via Inferno 3 and via Valdonica 14. Nowadays the ghetto is still attractively dark and mysterious but long-since secularized and home to a number of good restaurants. The ghetto and surrounding areas also contain many curious buildings such as la **Chiesa di San Giobbe**, a former church subsequently used as a hospital for sufferers of *mal francese* (literally 'French evil' or syphilis) and now subsumed within a pleasant shopping mall called the **Galleria Acquaderni** whose shops still bear the church's frescoes on some of their walls. Here are also to be found a number of the city's other surviving towers: the **Torre degli Uguzzoni** in vicolo Tubertini, the 11th-century **Torre Prendiparte** (59 m) in via Sant'Alo, also known as *la coronata* (crowned one) on account of its crenellations, the **Casa-torre Guidozagni**, near via Albriroli which was lowered in 1487 to its current height, and the **Torre degli Azzoguidi**, also known as *l'Altabella*, reputedly after a tall and fair Bolognese lady of the quarter, on via Caduti di Cefalonia.

Palazzo Malvezzi and Palazzo Magnani

Palazzo Malvezzi, via Zamboni 13; Palazzo Magnani, via Zamboni 20. *Map 4, C7, p256*

At the top of via Zamboni are a clutch of fine noble houses now variously the seat of banks and local government. The **Palazzo Malvezzi** is known for its grandiose staircase by Francesco Bibiena and the fine statue of Hercules, complete with club and lion at its entrance. Palazzo Magnani contains in its first floor drawing room arguably one of Bologna's finest art treasures, a cycle of 14 hectic and wonderfully animated and fantastical frescoes by Annibale Carracci, completed between 1588 and 1591, depicting the foundation of Rome, complete with satyrs, hermaphrodites and masks.

★ Chiesa di San Giacomo Maggiore

via Zamboni/piazza Rossini, **T** 051-225970. *Mon-Sun 0645-1300, 1600-1800. Map 4, B8, p256*

As with many of Bologna's churches, San Giacomo has undergone several additions and rebuildings over the centuries so that little is left of its Venetian-Gothic origins and it appears as a bit of a mish-mash of styles. Originally built in the mid-13th century, the church was appropriated in the 15th century by the Bentivoglio family, who made this area of the city their power base. Most of the revisions to the style and structure of the church were carried out on their orders. Perhaps the most striking of these is the beautiful pink side arcade. The recurring motif on the capitals is the seashell, symbol of the traveller and pilgrim San Giacomo (St James). The apse of the church still supports the remains of the second circle of the old city wall.

Within San Giacomo's Renaissance interior are many artistic treasures, most notable of which are *St Roch* by Ludovico Carracci, the tomb of Galeazzo Bentivoglio by Jacopo della Quercia and the Bentivoglio's own private chapel, the altar of which has some striking artwork by Lorenzo Costa depicting family victories over other Bolognese dynasties. The *Madonna Enthroned, Thanked by Giovanni II and his Wife Ginevra Sforza and their Children* is the eloquent and literal title of a painting by Lorenzo Costa specially commissioned by Giovanni II, the family Godfather, as a votive offering to thank the Almighty for their escape from an attempted massacre by the Malvezzi family. In addition to building towers, it was also fashionable to show your power by buying and decorating your own chapel. Costa's two paintings to the left of the above were the painter's ironic way of showing how hollow earthly fame becomes in death.

● *Above the arch leading into via del Carro beyond San Giacomo Maggiore is a mask from which wine flowed onto the crowd below on festive occasions.*

▶ La famiglia Bentivoglio – patrons of the arts

The Bentivoglio family was one of the great warring dynasties of medieval Bologna. At the height of their power in 1460, Sante Bentivoglio commissioned the construction of an immense family palace that stretched over most of the northern side of via Zamboni. Sante's son Giovanni II, though not an artist himself, was a keen appreciator of the arts and of beauty in general and it was during his 46-year reign that the arts flourished – in particular the school of Francesco Francia. The city also gained many of its more renowned embellishments at this time, especially in the University quarter, which was the family's stronghold (see San Giacomo Maggiore, p52).

A pact between the King of France and the Pope eventually led to Giovanni II's exile and overthrow. In the years that followed, all reminders of the Bentivoglio dynasty were destroyed, including their palace.

The family is perhaps best evoked these days in the famous jazz club that bears their name on via Mascarella and the trendy wine-bar, called Le Stanze del Tenente located in their former family chapel.

Oratorio di Santa Cecilia

piazza Rossini, via Zamboni 15 (entrance through portico Bentivolgio next to San Giacomo Maggiore). **T** 051 225970
1000-1300, 1500-1900 daily, free. Map 4, C8, p256

A great patron of the arts, the Bentivoglio Lord, Giovanni II, who ruled Bologna at the beginning of the 16th century, commissioned a large number of projects to embellish his city. Among them were the frescoes depicting the life of Santa Cecilia in this little oratory through the archway of San Giacomo, which were painted by some of the greatest artists living in the city at that time: Francesco

Francia, Lorenzo Costa and Amico Aspertini. Recently restored and opened to the public with new lighting, this is one of Bologna's real art treasures.

Teatro Comunale

via Zamboni 30/Largo Respighi 1, **T** 199-107070, www.comunalebologna.it *Map 4, B8, p256*

Bologna's city theatre was built in the 18th century on the site of the stables of the magnificent Bentivoglio palace, which had been razed to the ground when that dynasty was overthrown in 1507. It was designed by Antonio Bibiena, a member of the renowned Galli family of Italian theatre designers. The colosseum-like 'boxes' and the u-shaped arena were a favoured form at the time. The theatre opened in 1763 with a performance of Gluck's *Triumph of Clelia*. Guided tours in Italian and English take place on Sundays at 1000 and Mondays at 1100. Tours last around one hour and cost €7 per person. **T** 0347-3335791.

Conservatorio di Musica G B Martini and Museo Bibliografico Musicale

piazza Rossini 2, **T** 051-222997/221117. *0900-1300. Closed Sun. Entry free. Map 4, C7, p256*

Bologna played host to many famous Italian composers such as Verdi, Rossini and Puccini and its music conservatory was a place of study and composition for many others, among them Bellini, Gluck, Wagner and, briefly, Mozart. Just off piazza Rossini, the building is a former Augustine convent confiscated, like many, by Napoleon and put to other use. It is easy to see how the cloistered setting might have provided inspiration. The magnificent concert hall has a huge organ and a gallery of portraits of great composers, musicians and divas of bygone days. More important is the collection of autographed scripts and rare scores dating from the

16th to 18th centuries, including the original of *The Barber of Seville*, kept in the Liceo Musicale. There are also hundreds of portraits of JC Bach by Gainsborough, a portrait of Farinelli (a famous castrato) by Giaquinto and a beautiful canvas entitled *A Musical Library* by Giuseppe Crespi.

Musei di Palazzo Poggi

via Zamboni 31-33, **T** 051-259021/2099360. *Mon-Fri 0830-1730, Sat-Sun 0900-1830 for all museums. All free. Map 2, H11, p253*

The seat of Europe's oldest university was originally located in the Archiginnasio (p41) but was moved here in 1803 by Napoleon who wanted to bring all the city's proliferating faculties together in one place to create a kind of campus. This is the engine room of Bologna *la dotta* (Bologna the learned), the home of the university library and many of the university's main faculties and museums. The 16th-century building was the former home of the Poggi family. Although of humble origin, the family spent almost their entire wealth on the construction of the palace to signify their social ascent, following the election of Giovanni Poggi to cardinal in 1551.

The Palazzo Poggi houses a series of diverse museums reflecting the vast range of subjects that were pioneered at the university by its early pupils.

L'Accademia della Scienza is the university's science institute, whose lower rooms are decorated in frescoes representing Ulysses by Pellgrino Tibaldi. The entrance at number 33 leads into a pleasant courtyard with a statue to Hercules in its centre by Angelo Pio. The Aula Carducci has been preserved to show where Bologna's famous poet gave his lectures between 1860 and 1904.

Atop the Palazzo Poggi and accounting for its rather odd shape is **La Specola dell'Osservatorio Astronomico** and **Museo di Astronomia**, a tower that houses the university's observatory and museum of astronomy. The ancient instruments for the measuring and examination of the skies are evocative and fascinating for their rather Heath Robinson-esque appearance.

Although it may seem strange for a landlocked city, the **Museo delle Navi**, Bologna's maritime museum, is considered to be one of the most important in the world for its rare models of 17th- and 18th-century warships; their technological innovation and advancement has fascinated studying scientists.

The **Museo di Architettura Militare** places military developments in the context of scientific and technological advancements. Models of various forms of armament and toy soldiers are on display, plus early defence diagrams carved in beautiful marquetry.

Finally, and not necessarily uppermost in the average visitor's mind, the **Museo Ostretrico Giovanni Antonio Galli**, the university's obstetrics museum, has a wide range of 18th-century instruments and incredible life-size models by Galli in wax and wood demonstrating the different phases of pregnancy in order to prepare 18th-century midwives for every eventuality.

There are many other small museums of niche interest for real enthusiasts within Palazzo Poggi and also dotted among the university faculties and lecture rooms behind the palazzo, along largo Trombetti, via Belmeloro and via Selmi. These specialist institutions are not necessarily a high priority for most visitors but include comparative anatomy, anatomy of pets and anthropology. The zoology museum is worth a look if you're into dead fish, birds and sea-shells or want to see a stuffed rhinoceros. A complete list of these museums can be found in the museums listing (p97).

!
•
The poet Dante Alighieri was one of Bologna university's most illustrious students. He is known to have taken a keen interest in science and in particular in astronomy. It is thought that the structure and mechanics of his *Divina Commedia* are likely to have been inspired by his student years.

Museo di Geologia e Paleontologia
via Zamboni 63, **T** 051-2094555. *Mon-Fri 0900-1230.*
Map 2, H12, p253

The university's other main collection of faculties and museums is across the road from Palazzo Poggi further down towards the decaying 13th-century gate of Porta San Donato. The best of these museums is Italy's largest museum of paleontology, containing over 1000 pieces, of which the most appealing (especially to children) will be one of only four existing examples in Europe of the friendly but enormous diplodocus dinosaur, 26 m long and 4 m tall. A full listing of other museums in this building can be found on p97.

Orto Botanico and l'Erbario
via Irnerio 42, **T** 051-2091280, *Mon-Fri 0800-1500;* l'Erbario
T 051-351304, *Mon-Fri 0830-1230;* Palazzina della Viola, via Filippo Re. *Map 2, F11, p253*

After streets of constant and intensive museum-visiting, the botanical gardens and herbarium make for a relaxing break. At two hectares, this geometrically beautiful garden of soothing lawns is a favourite for lounging students hanging out between lectures. Founded in 1658, it is home to over 5000 species of local and exotic species of plant, while the Herbarium has specimens of over 110,000 dried plants. The adjoining **Palazzina della Viola**, named after the violets of Giovanni II Bentivoglio's gardens nearby, is now the home of the university's faculty of agriculture.

Museo di Anatomia Umana
via Irnerio 48 **T** 051-276811. *Mon-Sat 0900-1200, free.*
Map 2, G12, p253

On a leafy boulevard, the museum of anatomy is Bologna's answer to Madame Tussaud's, the difference being that the waxworks here were created in the pursuit of scientific knowledge and, specifically, the practice of dissection, the body being far easier to understand "with the eyes than with the ears" as its founder, Pope Benedict XIV said. It is not necessarily the place you thought you'd end up on a visit to the city but the models, all hand sculpted as opposed to moulded, are of an exquisite accuracy and beauty, important in their own right as objects of art but also in demonstrating the services of art to science.

★ La Pinacoteca Nazionale
via delle Belle Arti 56, **T** 051-4209411/4211984, www.pinacotecabologna.it. *Tue-Sun, 0900-1900, closed Mon. Entry €4, €3 with museum card, concessions €2. Free for under 18s and over 60s.* Map 2, G/H11, p253

Bologna's National Gallery is a must for lovers and historians of art but also provides an insight into the important role Bologna played in the cultural development of Italy – a fact that can sometimes be obscured by the allure of more famous art treasures elsewhere in the country. The gallery has the largest collection of canvasses by artists from the influential 17th-century Bolognese school, among them Tibaldi, Reni, the Carracci brothers and Guercino, some late Titian, and also some masterpieces from preceding centuries including a polyptych by Giotto and *St George and the Dragon* by Vitale di Bologna. The gallery was founded by Napoleon as part of his programme for cultural reform and the collection was based on a set of donations to Pope Clement VII. To this Napoloeon added all the art he was able to confiscate from the various churches, convents and monasteries he suppressed during his occupation. In so doing his vision was to unify the canvasses (now located in a suppressed Jesuit convent) with the Accademia delle Belle Arti next door – a logical union of the practice of art and examples of its perfection. Napoleon's reforms did not stop many of the works of art ending up in the Louvre, some of which have since been returned.

Nuovo Palazzo Bentivoglio

via delle Belle Arti 8. *Closed to public except courtyard.*
Map 2, H9, p253

Having destroyed the magnificent Bentivoglio palace in 1507, it
seems the citizens of Bologna repented their hasty overthrow of
the dynasty who had held such power in the 15th century and
whose patronage had embellished so much of their city. This
imposing structure built in swift homage in the mid-16th century
by Tibaldi is a suggestive reminder of their former hegemony
although today it is home to less lordly residents and small
businesses. The unfinished courtyard exudes an atmosphere of
neglect but it is worth a look for its beautiful Romanesque
double loggias.

Chiesa di San Martino

via Oberdan 25. *0700-1300, 1500-1830.* *Map 4, A6, p256*

Stranded between the university district and via
dell'Indipendenza, this little church with its tranquil piazza is
often ignored in favour of the city's bigger attractions. The recent
discovery of a fragment of a fresco by Paolo Uccello depicting
the Nativity in the first left-hand chapel may change this,
although other masterpieces have been found inside, notably
the *Adoration of the Magi* in the Boncompagni family chapel by
Aspertini. Begun in the early 13th century, in the face of much
resistance by the Augustine monks of San Giacomo nearby, this
is one of few examples in Bologna of a church that has not been
tampered with through the ages and remains much as it was,
save for the 19th-century façade. The church used to be accessed
by crossing a small bridge over a weir, which has since been
covered up.

Palazzo Grassi

via Marsala 12. *Closed to the public.* Map 2, H8, p253

With its Tudor-like wooden porticoes and beams, this is a rare and beautifully intact vestige of 13th-century Bologna and one of the city's oldest buildings. The wooden porticoes also remain on the buildings opposite making this a very picturesque little back-corner of the city.

Via delle Moline and Bologna's canals

Map 2, G8-H9, p253

Unlike most big cities Bologna was not built on a river and thus had to divert water from elsewhere. In the 12th century a canal was built to divert water from the westerly river Reno to the city centre. The water served not only for sanitation and refreshment but also, through the watermills after which via delle Moline is named, for power to fuel the silk and hemp industries that were Bologna's main medieval commercial activities. Up until the early 20th century the canal also served as a transportation vehicle for the import of essential goods to the city. The Reno is connected to the Po in the north enabling the transport of Veronese marble and other materials for the construction and embellishment of the city. The canal lock at Casalecchio west of Bologna used to be one of the city's most picturesque spots until suburban sprawl and modern transportation methods dictated that the canals fell into disuse and were covered over by roads. Although it may seem unlikely, water still flows through the foundations of old Bologna but it is still visible in only a few places, most notably the bridge on via Piella opposite which is a peep-hole into the watery past, and between via Capo di Lucca and via Alessandrini. This area has been ambitiously referred to as Bologna's Little Venice. The comparison is odious, as this poor, working-class quarter has a seedy, medieval quality all of its own.

Piazza VIII Agosto

Map 2, F8, p253

Named after the battle in which the Bolognese repelled the attentions of the invading Austrians in the First War of Italian Independence in 1848, this square looks for five days a week like an ugly and anonymous car park at odds with the city's prevailing aesthetics. Also known as La Piazzola, on Fridays and Saturdays it turns into a huge and colourful market which draws locals and bargain hunters from the provinces in their droves. Wares on offer range from shoes, gloves and other leather goods to books, china and various household items. The simultaneous bric-a-brac market is up the steps in the Giardini della Montagnola.

Giardini Pubblici della Montagnola

Open all day, closed at night. Times vary according to season.
Map 2, E8, p253

Thanks to all its porticoes and cobbled streets Bologna can seem like a city of unrelenting stone, unsoothed by nature and open spaces. An aerial view shows that many of the city's green spaces are closed off from street-level view by the palazzi and courtyards which surround them. The public Montagnola Gardens represent the largest green space inside the Centro Storico. They were landscaped by Giambattista Martinetti in 1806 on the mound created by the excavations and ruins of the papal castle, Castello di Galliera, of which a ruin still remains at their northern end. A grand set of steps leads up into the gardens at the foot of which is a dramatic and sensuous statue to Venus and Neptune by Diego Sarti. On Fridays and Saturdays the gardens host a vast flea-market, popular with dedicated peddlers and idle browsers.

Via San Vitale
Map 3, A9-B12, p255

With its preponderance of expensive antique shops and galleries, via San Vitale is more sedate nowadays than the bohemian university hangouts of via Zamboni and via delle Belle Arti. In Roman times it was known as the *via Salaria* as it led out towards the salt mines at Cervia, beyond Ravenna. Consisting of one almost continuous portico on both sides, the road is lined with many fine palazzi open to the public, notably the **Palazzo Orsi** at number 28 which is full of interesting and dramatic Baroque statues and painted ceilings, and the fortress-like **Palazzo Fantuzzi** with elephant motifs in its façade at number 23, which has a beautiful staircase lined with statues. At number 56 is the **Palazzo Scagliarini-Rossi**, 19th-century home of Cornelia Rossi, the beautiful wife of the landscape architect Martinetti who is said to have 'surrounded' herself with the intelligentsia and artists of the time, including Byron, and held legendary parties. The atmospheric road of **via Broccaindosso** was one of the homes of the poet Carducci at number 20.

Torresotto
At the midway point of via San Vitale. *Map 3, A10, p255*

This tower is a rare survivor of the 16 gates that were built in the late 12th century as Bologna's second ring of defence against Emperor Frederick I (Barbarossa). The crenellated wall ran for 4 km around the city with an average height of 8 m.

Chiesa di Santi Vitale e Agricola
via San Vitale 48. *0700-1300, 1500-1830. Map 4, C8, p256*

This is a Romanesque church to Bologna's first martyrs, the return of whose relics from the occupying Franks coincided closely with the foundation of the post-Roman city. It is most notable for the paintings in its chapel and a beautiful crypt. Vitale and Agricola are said to have been killed on this spot by the Emperor Diocletian during the Christian persecutions.

Southeast: Santo Stefano and around

*Fed by the attractive capillaries of **via Santo Stefano** and **via Castiglione**, the beauty of this area is nowhere more evident than in the triangular **piazza Santo Stefano**, site of the intricate complex of churches of the same name, one of the great architectural and artistic wonders of the city. The important **strada Maggiore**, once part of the Roman via Emilia, witnessed the coming and going, the coronation and invasions of alternate patriarchs and popes. These left their mark on this quarter of the city in a dense forestation of statements. From luxurious palaces and gardens (sadly closed to the public) to exquisite churches and sanctuaries such as **Santa Maria dei Servi** and the **Basilica of Santo Domenico**, all are home to countless masterpieces of the decorative arts. Narrow and shadowy in contrast, via Castiglione leads up to the murky backwater of the **Mirasoli** district, whose dark, faceless streets still exude the stench of the suspicion that reigned many hundreds of years ago, now replaced by the cheer of some of the best, but least-visited, restaurants in town.*

▸▸ *See Sleeping p122, Eating and drinking p144, Bars and clubs p173*

◉ Sights

Loggia della Mercanzia
piazza della Mercanzia. Access to entrance hall only
Map 4, D6, p256

Today housing the Chamber of Commerce, the late 14th-century former customs house, designed by the architect di Vicenzo in the city's traditional red and white livery, is one of the finest Gothic buildings in Bologna. Having suffered significant damage during the Allied bombardments, its florid windows and extravagant balcony, from which merchants' decisions were announced to the populace, have been lovingly restored. Also of note are the clock and the buliding's many niches full of statues to saints and symbols of civic justice.

● *To the right of the Loggia della Mercanzia is an inscription to make any modern-day student jealous. Roughly translated it states that in recognition of the importance of the city's university, students shall have free books, clothes and food.*

Palazzo Bolognini
via Santo Stefano 9-11. *Map 4, E6, p256*

Further up via Santo Stefano from the Loggia della Mercanzia is the former house of another of Bologna's powerful families, the Bolognini. Built in the 16th century, the building is also known as the *palazzo delle teste* (the palace of heads) on account of the many clay busts that look down onto the street and which have been attributed to the sculptor Alfonso Lombardi.

Le Case Isolani and La Corte Isolani
Map 4, E6-7, p256

An elegant passageway links via Santo Stefano to the strada Maggiore via a series of courtyards, which, in the way they are decorated, represent a journey from the Middle Ages to the Renaissance. At either end are two houses named after the merchants who plied Cypriot wares here in the 13th century (*isolani* literally means 'from the islands'). The house on the side of piazza Santo Stefano has a marvellous spiral staircase by Vignola leading up to rooms adorned with many fine paintings by 17th- and 18th-century Bolognese artists. The house on the Strada Maggiore side (no.19) is characterized by a spectacular 10-m high

Neptune's fountain
The huge Fontana del Nettuno offers tourists the perfect photo opportunity.

1 The huge statue of Pope Gregory XIII on the façade of the Palazzo Comunale demonstrated the papacy's power in the city at the end of the 16th century.
▶▶ See page 34.

2 Cycling is an excellent way to explore Bologna's narrow and (almost) traffic-free streets.
▶▶ See page 25.

3 The Palazzo Archiginnasio was the once the seat of the university. Its rose-coloured arcades are typical of the city.
▶▶ See page 41.

4 Locals will tell you that 'la cucina bolognese' is the best in Italy. Stuffed pasta dishes, such as lasagne, are the city's speciality.
▶▶ See pages 132 and 137.

5 As well as feasting on Parma's famous cheese and ham, don't miss the city's 11th-century cathedral. ▶▶ See page 104.

6 Rimini's beaches make a welcome change from all that sightseeing – as long as you can find a space on the sand.
▶▶ See page 114.

Due Torri
The 12th-century Torre degli Asinelli and Torre Garisenda loom over the church of San Bartolomeo in the heart of Bologna.

Shady arcades
Enjoy the shifting perspectives of ancient buildings, as they are framed by Bologna's arcaded streets.

Fashion forward
The streets around Bologna's piazza Maggiore are lined with enough chic and offbeat boutiques to satisfy even the fussiest fashionista.

Glutton's delight
In Bologna's lively Mercato di Mezzo, butchers, greengrocers and delicatessens sell the fresh ingredients for the city's renowned cuisine.

La Rossa

From above, it's clear how Bologna gained its nickname - the red one.

Mosaic town
The Battistero is one of many buildings in Ravenna to be decorated with exquisite Byzantine mosaics.

Lest we forget
The walls of Bologna's Palazzo Comunale are lined with photographs of resistance partisans massacred by the Nazis at the end of World War II.

wooden portico. Today the passageway in between is home to
boutiques, banks, restaurants and cafés.

● *If you crane your neck and peer up in to the murky wooden
darkness under the portico of strada Maggiore 19, you can see two
mysterious wooden arrows sticking into the ceiling. Much mythology
surrounds the origins of these arrows (of which there were once three)
but the most probable explanation is that they were put there in jest
by builders restoring the portico in the 19th century when the two
supporting pillars were added.*

Via Santo Stefano
Map 3, B8-G12, p255

Along via Santo Stefano are many fine noble houses, which conceal
lovely courtyards behind their gates. The pavement is uneven in
parts reputedly due to rich families wanting to distinguish their
addresses from neighbours'. At number 31 is the old **Teatro Corso**,
inaugurated by Napoloeon, which witnessed the debut of the young
composer, Gioacchino Rossini. At number 33 is the **Palazzo
Finzi-Contini**, which used to house the *albergo del Corso*, where the
novelist Giorgio Bassani stayed, a sojourn that may have inspired his
novel *Nel Giardino dei Finzi-Contini* (actually set in Ferrara). A plaque
on the exterior wall commemorates another famous guest of the
albergo, the romantic poet, Giacomo Leopardi.

Piazza Santo Stefano
Map 4, E7, p256

Surrounded by intriguing and beautiful buildings, this piazza is one
of Bologna's most picturesque locations. Triangular in shape, the
cobbled square is paved with lines of flat, grey stones, an aesthetic
device in conflict with classical ideas of symmetry but intended
when coming into the piazza from the north to lead the eye
towards the church at the piazza's southern end.

★ Chiesa di Santo Stefano
via Santo Stefano 24, **T** 051-223256, www.abbaziasantostefano.it
Daily 0900-1200, 1530-1830. Map 4, F7, p256

Along with the Basilica of San Petronio and the Due Torri, this church is one of the must-sees for any visitor to Bologna. At its peak it was a Russian doll of seven interlinked churches within churches. Its fifth-century circular core built around a natural spring was constructed by Bishop Petronius, soon-to-be patron saint of Bologna, on the site of a temple to the pagan goddess Isis. The complex is sometimes referred to as La Santa Gerusalemme after the seven connecting sanctuaries in the Holy City. Petronius is supposed to have brought back a copy of the design from a fifth-century trip to Palestine.

The church is rumoured to be named after the Christian martyr St Stephen, whose remains were found in Jerusalem around the same time. Although the precise evolution of the building is not known, it is thought that the additions and expansions were added variously by the occupying Lombards and then the Benedictine and Celestine monks between 983 and 1493. The complex was restored between 1870 and 1930, causing some inexplicable demolition and the reduction of the number of churches to the current four.

The first and principal church is the **Chiesa del Santissimo Crocefisso** to which the restorations returned its Lombardic medieval aspect. The beautiful crypt is composed of columns, capitals and other materials from the original Roman construction and bears a pagan inscription to Isis.

The **Basilica dei Santi Vitale e Agricola** is thought to be Bologna's oldest Christian church, again built from the original pagan construction with 11th-century Lombardic naves, and housing the sarcopoghi of the two martyrs of Bologna from which it takes its name. The tranquil *cortile di Pilato* is named after the Lombardic facsimile of Pontius Pilate's bowl in its centre (where he 'washed his hands' of Christ).

▶ **San Petronio**

In the fifth century, during the decline of the Roman Empire, Bologna fell into ruin as all the political and administrative infrastructure disappeared. Petronius was a local bishop at the time about whom little is known, other than that he was a follower of Saint Ambrosius, the patron saint of Milan. Legend, however, has credited Petronius with rescuing Bologna from terminal decline by defining the city's boundaries and embarking upon the design and construction of a number of buildings, ensuring the city's continued protection and development. Most notable of these buildings is the complex of interlinked churches of Santo Stefano, inspired by a similar design that Petronius brought back from a pilgrimage to Palestine and the Holy City.

It was not until the Middle Ages, as Bologna developed its university and resilient civic spirit, that her citizens began to seek a symbol of their origins with which they could identify. The result of their collective root-searching was to elevate their mysterious saviour-bishop to the status of patron saint.

To the north is the **Chiesa del San Sepolcro** (*closed 1200-1530*) which contains the bones of St Petronius (except the skull which is in the basilica). Note a charming image of an angel atop the empty tomb of Christ with dozing soldiers and the women who discovered Christ's disappearance. At Easter the sepulchre is opened to allow people in to recreate the discovery of the Resurrection.

To the west is the **Chiesa della Trinita**, virtually unrecognisable as a church after the restorations, but housing a beautiful fresco of the *Adoration of the Magi* by Simone de' Crocefissi. Beyond this is the peaceful Romanesque cloister with a beautifully harmonious double loggia supported by capitals playfully decorated with sculpted animals, built by the Benedictines in the 11th century. A small **museum** contains various works of art recovered during the restoration works showing the evolution of Bolognese and Italian painting, most notably the 13th-century *Massacre of the Innocents* in the left-hand room.

Chiesa di Santa Maria dei Servi
strada Maggiore, **T** 051-226807. *0700-1145, 1545-1945.*
Map 3, C10-11, p255

Despite the rude intrusion of nearby traffic, one cannot fail to be affected by the delicacy and fragility of the *quadriportico* (four-sided arcade) that stands before this church. There was originally only one side arcade, built in 1393. The completion of the square was one of the few beautiful interventions of the 19th century, although it came at the cost of demolishing the church of San Tommaso, which had, for hundreds of years, stood in its centre. Inside, the church is no less special and is best known as the site of a *Madonna and Child* by Cimabue and some 14th-century frescoes by Lippo di Dalmasio and Vitale da Bologna, although these should not obscure the many 17th- and 18th-century Bolognese school paintings which are mostly to be found in the sacristy and convent. At Christmas time the Santa Lucia fair, with Nativity figures, Christmas tree and toys, is held in the quadrangle.

Chiesa di San Giovanni in Monte
via Monticelli. *Mon-Sun 0800-1200, 1500-1800. Map 3, C9, p255*

More of a gallery than a church, this raised 13th-century building with a 15th-century Venetian façade contains a stunning collection of paintings within its Gothic interior, including works by Guercino, Francesco del Cossa and the Crowning of the Virgin altarpiece by

Lorenzo Costa. In the middle of the central nave is the bizarre sight of an upturned old Roman Corinthian column topped by a cross in a symbol of Christianity's victory over paganism. The majestic terracotta eagle, symbol of St John, in the lunetta above the wooden door, is by Niccolo dell'Arca.

Piazza San Domenico
Map 3, D7, p255

This peaceful square laid with river pebbles has a distinct rural feel and also serves as a showcase for a number of important monuments such as the 14th-century elevated tomb to Rolandino de' Passegeri, one of the city's Notaries and a founding father of European law and human rights who is remembered for his heroic resistance to Frederick II in the name of freedom and democracy. The piazza's two columns support statues to the Virgin in celebration of the end of the plague in 1632 and to San Domenico, the latter being sculpted according to a drawing by Guido Reni.

★ Chiesa di San Domenico
piazza San Domenico. **T** 051-6400411. *Daily 0700-1300, 1530-1930. Map 3. D7/8, p255*

Begun in 1221 to commemorate the life of Domingo de Guzman, the founder of the Dominican order, this church contains one of the masterpieces of Bolognese heritage, the Fabergé-esque *arca* or canopy to Nicola Pisano's tomb of the saint in the right-hand nave, designed and carved by Niccolo de Bari; the beauty of the canopy earned him the name Niccolo dell'Arca. He died before all the statuettes had been completed, leaving the outstanding work – the figures of St Petronius and St Procolus – to no less a hand than Michelangelo. Michelangelo also carved the prominent kneeling angel on the front – a detail that has sold a lot of postcards for the city. Among the bas-reliefs on the ark is a little dog. The dog motif is also repeated on the plinth below the sarcophagus. Legend has it that before his birth, Domenico's mother had a vision that she would give birth to a dog that would spread light and happiness in the name of the Lord. As with many of the city's churches, additions were made in the form of lavish side chapels to the vanity of various ruling families, decorated with superb frescoes by Ludovico Carracci, di Dalmasio, Filippino Lippi (*The Mystic Marriage of St Catherine*), Guido Reni (*The Glory of St Dominic* – above the 'arca') and other masters of the Bolognese school. Guido Reni is buried in the Rosario chapel in the church. The nearby convent is composed of two cloisters: the first, the cloister *dei Morti* (of the Dead) is noted for its Roman-Gothic belltower; the other for being the cell, home and deathbed of the saint himself. There is also a small **museum** beyond the apse of the main basilica (*Tue-Sun 1000-1200, 1500-1800, free*).

Conservatorio and Chiesa della Madonna del Baraccano
piazza del Baracano 2, **T** 051-392680. *Sat-Sun 1000-1300, 1600-1900.* *Map 3, F11, p255*

Set into the remains of the third and outer circle of the old city walls, this church is famous for the 15th-century portico through which it is accessed. The building above the portico is the seat of the Conservatorio del Baraccano, which was established in 1531 as a kind of finishing school for less well-off young girls. The church itself was commissioned by Giovanni Bentivoglio in 1472 to subsume a small chapel that bears an image of the Madonna set in the city walls. Ever preoccupied with beauty, various additions including the cupola were made in the 15th and 16th centuries to enhance the overall aesthetic effect.

Strada Maggiore
Map 3, B9-C12, p255

This important street, a suburban section of the Roman via Emilia, is lined with a series of former noble residences. At number 24 the **casa Sampieri** has paintings by all three Carraccis in the three ground floor rooms with ceilings by Guercino. At number 44 the imposing **palazzo Bargellini** is recognisable by the enormous, sinuous and muscular statues of Atlas that stand on either side of the entrance supporting the balcony above (the Greek god Zeus condemned Atlas to support the weight of the world on his shoulders for having colluded with the Titans' plot to overthrow him). This building houses the **Davia Bargellini** fine-art collection (**T** 051-236708, *Tue-Sun 0900-1400, free*) which includes many famous masterpieces from the 14th through to the 18th century by both Crespis and Donato Creti. Art pilgrims will not want to miss the *Madonna and Child* and deeply moving Pieta by Simone dei Crocefissi. The same building also houses the **Museo d'Arte Industriale** (which, translated, would be Museum of Applied Arts) which displays furniture and decorative art from various eras and provides a window onto middle-class and noble Bolognese interiors dating from the 16th to the 18th centuries (details as above). Just off strada Maggiore, via Fondazza 37 was where the artist Giorgio Morandi lived (see p37), among the colours that inspired his soft abstract paintings. At number 11 is an interior design shop in which a piece of the old via Emilia Roman road has been uncovered, complete with the grooves made by wheels.

Palazzo Ercolani

strada Maggiore 45. *Map 3, C11, p255*

This 18th-century building is a senatorial palace once inhabited by the Ercolani family, who were part of the senate when the city was under papal rule. Beyond the courtyard is a classically English garden, while an arcade leads to a statue-lined staircase up to rooms that are now used as part of the university's Faculty of Political Science.

Casa Carducci
piazza Carducci, **T** 051-225583/347592. *Tue-Sun 0900-1300, Thu 0900-1700. Closed Mon. €2.58, concessions €1.25.*
Map 3, E12, p251

His earlier more humble lodgings being in via Broccaindosso, the poet Carducci was given this 16th-century residence as a new home by Queen Margherita of Savoy with whom he was head over heels in love. Carducci lived here from 1890 until his death in 1907, when his vast collection of books, letters and manuscripts was donated by the Queen to the citizens of Bologna in the form of the Carducci library. The building was erected on the ruins of the medieval outer city wall and since 1990 has been home also to the **Museo Civico del Risorgimento**, a museum celebrating the creation of the unifed Italian state in 1860. In celebration of the poet's love of nature, the house also has a garden, *il giardino monumentale* (monument garden), so-called after its central statue to the poet by Leonardo Bistolfi.

Via Castiglione
Map 3, B8-F9, p255

The name of this road is supposedly an elision of the words *castello* (castle) and *leone* (lion). In this instance the lion was the powerful Pepoli family (see p73) and the many buildings they owned on this road constituted their fortress.

Palazzo Pepoli and Palazzo Pepoli Campogrande
Palazzo Pepoli, via Castiglione 6-10; Palazzo Pepoli Campogrande, via Castiglione 7. *Map 4, E6, p256*

The Palazzo Pepoli, with its Guelph crenellations displaying the appropriate aspect of a fortress, was commissioned in 1344 by Taddeo Pepoli as a sign of power to the citizens of Bologna.

> ### Taddeo Pepoli

Bologna's history is populated by individuals and families that at one time or other held sway over the city between periods of papal rule and outside occupation. Taddeo Pepoli, a vicar by calling, dominated public life in the tumultuous years between 1337 and 1344 owing to his skill in the art of diplomacy between Guelph and Ghibellines. Other members of the Pepoli family continued to have great influence in the region until the end of the 18th century.

Opposite is an equally impressive piece of Pepoli vanity on an even greater scale, this time commissioned by a different generation, Eduardo Pepoli in the late 17th century. Less of a fortress, this was conceived as a place for receptions, banquets and festivals. Inside are many fine frescoes, some of them forcibly paying homage to the Pepolis, while the most spectacular are the 17th-century paintings by Giuseppe Maria Crespi depicting *The Allegory of the Seasons*, *The Triumph of Hercules* and *The Council of the Gods*.

Ex-Chiesa e Convento di Santa Lucia
via Castiglione 36. *Map 3, D8, p255*

Relieved of its religious functions by Napoleon, this 17th-century church and convent was designed by Girolamo Rinaldi on the site of the 13th-century original. Set back from the porticoed road, it boasts another of Bologna's unfinished façades, with a bare and stubbly charcoal face resembling a climbing wall. It is now the *Aula Magna* (main lecturing hall) of the university, decorated with a famous Madonna by Giuseppe Mazza and inaugurated in 1988 by Pope John Paul II on the 800th anniversary of the city university.

Palazzo di Giustizia
piazza del Tribunale. *Map 3, E7, p255*

Bologna's law courts stand majestically, as if in judgement
themselves, looking over the flowery piazza del Tribunale.
Originally a 16th-century commission as a private residence,
the building has undergone numerous additions and restorations,
the most notable being the harmonious façade, the central section
of which has been attributed to Palladio, and the rest to Tibaldi.
Restoration has also preserved the elegant staircase, the courtyard
and a number of fine canvasses on the first floor by Franceschini,
Bigari and Giani.

Piazza Galvani
Map 4, F3, p256

Just in front of the Archiginnasio, this piazza is named after the
19th-century Bolognese scientist, Luigi Galvani, who conducted
ground-breaking experiments in electricity using frogs and from
whom we get the word 'galvanize'. The statue in the square shows
him peering into a book with a petrified frog on the page.

Piazza Minghetti
Map 4, F5, p256

This leafy square, flanked by the imposing main post office
building, is named after Marco Minghetti, one of the architects of
the unification of Italy, who became the young nation's Home
Secretary in its 1860 Turin Parliament. Bizarrely, he pursued a
policy of local government that diced with all the regions' old local
rivalries. He was responsible for liberating Rome from Napoloeon
III but was forced to resign when he tried to move the capital from
Turin to Florence.

Mirasoli
Map 3, E6, p254

Literally translated as 'reflecting the sun' and so named after the reflection cast by a nearby branch of the then uncovered city canal, the group of alleys between via Miramonte and via d'Azeglio was once one of the dodgiest parts of town; a little Sicily, complete with its own code of honour and culture of *omerta* – see nothing, hear nothing, say nothing – people here feared to tread lest they be knifed. It was correspondingly colourful, with many notorious *osterie*, most of which no longer exist, although Osteria le Mura (p147) still provides a hint of the area's disaffected past.

Chiesa di San Procolo
via Massimo d'Azeglio 52, **T** 051-331223. *0800-1100, 1700-1900.* Map 3, D6, p255

This diminutive church built on the site of an old Roman temple has a 13th-century crypt where Proculus, the eponymous Roman soldier was entombed, but not before becoming a saint for having dared profess his Christian faith to his superior officer in the Imperial army. It has undergone many incarnations since then, and even served as a warehouse in Napoleonic times, before being restored as a place of worship in 1826. It has become famous for a piece of early graffiti, a cryptic ancient tongue-twister inscribed on the left façade: 'Si procul a Proculo Proculi campana fuisset, nunc procula a Proculo Proculis ipse forret, A.D. 1393'. Roughly translated it means 'If Proculus' bell was far from Proculus, then Proculus would be far from Proculus' Legend has it that Proculus (the Second) was a bell-ringer who died after being crushed by a falling bell.

Southwest: around via del Pratello

*The southwest of the Centro Storico contrasts the elegant **via d'Azeglio**, catwalk and hunting ground for Bologna's dedicated followers of fashion among wallet-bruising boutiques, with the boozy uproarious osterie of the **via del Pratello** and **via San Felice**, famous for their concentration of years-old drinking holes and for the concentration of their house distillations. Amid these extremes are the leafy squares of **piazza Galvani** and **piazza Malpighi**, the latter providing the setting for the stronghold of the Franciscan order in Bologna in the imposing and unusual form of the **Chiesa di San Francesco**. The important artery of **via Saragozza** leads past the **Collegio di Spagna**, symbol of Bologna's early cosmopolitan outlook. It continues back in time, past many old bars and cafés, full of locals and unchanged for decades, up to the **porta Saragozza**, gateway to the city's great colonnaded pilgrimage site on the hill, the **Santuario di San Luca**.*

▸▸ *See Sleeping p123, Eating and drinking p149, Bars and clubs p174*

◉ Sights

Collegio di Spagna
via del Collegio di Spagna. **T** 051-330408. *Only the courtyard can be visited.* Map 3, C5, p254

Even in the 14th century the world's famous universities were cosmopolitan and open to overseas students. This building, one of Bologna's more unusual pieces of architecture due to the Hispanic colour and style of its charming double loggia courtyard, was built to house students from Spain (known as *los Bolonios*). The building was a project of the Archbishop of Toledo, briefly a papal minister of the city before being overthrown by the council. In 1364, having paid in advance for a lavish funeral, he bequeathed the rest of his fortune in a will that requested the building of a college to house

24 Spanish students from noble families. It is said that these students and their successors enjoyed impunity from the law as they were subjects of the Spanish crown.

Piazza Malpighi
Map 3, A4, p254

Formerly a part of piazza San Francesco, this is Bologna's most colourful square, flanked down one side by a frescoed arcade that used to form part of the church of San Francesco nearby. The column in the centre supports a bronze statue of the Immaculate Conception, designed by Guido Reni. The Bolognese place flowers. at the statue's feet on 8th December every year at the *Festa della Concezione Immacolata*.

Chiesa di San Francesco
piazza San Francesco, **T** 051-221762. *Mon-Sun 0630-1200, 1500-1900. Map 3, A4, p254*

Completed between 1236 and 1263, this church and its convent was established as the HQ of the Franciscan order following their arrival in the city in 1211. It is a fine, towering example of Gothic architecture with a French influence; a heavy and complex forest of spidery flying buttresses, which may or may not appeal. Considering that it was badly damaged in World War II, and also used by Napoleon as a depot and customs house, it has been successfully restored. The interior, supported by octagonal trunk-like columns, conceals a number of important works of art: the beautiful marble altarpiece conceived by the Masegne brothers in Venice in 1392, depicting scenes from the life of St Francis, and the pyramidal mausoleums to *i glossari*, the university's founding lecturers and legal scholars, in the peaceful cloister of the convent next door. Set behind the altar is an unusual semi-circle of chapels notable for a tryptych completed in 1929 by the sculptress, Teresa Gruber.

Via del Pratello
Map 3, A2-4, p254

This road and the working-class area between via Sant'Isaia and via San Felice has always been renowned for its concentration of *osterie* and still today is a buzzing area thick with door-to-door dodgy dives and drinking joints. A Bolognese version of Barcelona's *ramblas*, at night it comes to life with street art, theatre and drunks.

Porta Saragozza
Map 3, C2, p254

With its three crenellated towers this is easily the most magnificent of the 10 gates of the outer city. However, its fine state of repair is the result of a reconstruction in 1857, which essentially followed the design of the original but could not resist a number of 19th-century embellishments, designed to herald the gateway to the famous cloistered path to the Santuario di San Luca on the hill.

Chiesa del Corpus Domini
via Tagliapietre 19, **T** 051-331277. *1000-1400, 1600-1800.*
Map 3, D5, p254

Also dedicated to Santa Caterina, Bologna's most important female saint, this little church and convent, restored to something like its former glory following considerable damage in the Second World War, has a beautiful portal and also a number of frescoes by Ludovico Carracci and friends inside.

Palazzo Albergati
via Saragozza 26-28. *Map 3, D3, p254*

Situated just before the city gate this palatial 16th-century building, distinguishable by the beautiful sandstone figures that embellish its façade, is thought at one stage to have housed Roman public baths during the reign of Augustus. Inside is a beautiful frieze by Lazzarino Casario.

Palazzo Bevilacqua

via Massimo d'Azeglio 31-33. *Map 3, C6, p254*

Seat of meetings of the Council of Trent in the 16th century, this building is a good example of Renaissance Bolognese architecture, with portals finely decorated in bas-relief and an elegant iron-balustraded balcony. Through the courtyard is an intriguing fountain with a lion spouting water from the top of a column.

Teatro Romano

via de' Carbonesi 7. *Map 3, C6, p254*

The partial remains of a Roman theatre, estimated to date back to 80 BC, were discovered under what is now the Bolognese branch of the department store, Coin. An unusual feature for any shop.

Chiesa di San Paolo Maggiore

via de' Carbonesi 18, **T** 051-331490. *0800-1100, 1700-1900. Map 3, C6, p254*

This early 17th-century church, with beautiful statuettes in the upper niches of the façade, also contains fresco masterpieces, particularly in the cupola and also *Paradise* by Ludovico Carracci and *St Gregory and the Souls of Purgatory* by Guercino. The façade features many swords, as it was commissioned by Cardinal Bernardino Spada (*spada* means sword).

Via Barberia

Map 3, B4-C5, p254

Via Barberia is lined with many fine *palazzi* from the 16th and 17th centuries: **Palazzo Marescotti** at number 4 is currently the home of the Italian Communist Party, a cause close to Bologna's heart, and contains a splendid staircase with double banister, designed by Giacomo Monti, as well as fine paintings; at number 13, **Palazzo Salina** has decorations from the 18th century; and in the corner of piazza Malpighi, where the second circle of the old city wall used to stand, **Palazzo Rusconi** has a façade embellished by rococo ornamentations.

Northwest: around via Galliera

*Badly damaged both by Allied bombardments and by subsequent bad taste in its reconstruction, the area to the northwest of piazza Maggiore is not instantly as attractive as the rest of the Centro Storico. With some notable exceptions, this is an area of modern urban planning, where wider boulevards replace the winding narrow alleys and concrete, glass and shiny marble replace the ageing red stone, wooden beams and porticoes. The more elegant, older central streets of **via Galliera**, **via Nazario Sauro** and **via Montegrappa** are home to beautiful, understated churches such as the exquisite **Chiesa della Madonna Colombano**, less bombastic than others in the city, as well as to the important **Museo Civico Medioevale e del Rinascimento**. Much of the area's interest lies beneath the surface in the warehouses and docks of the city's ancient system of underground canals. In recent years, these forgotten industrial spaces, especially in the areas around **Porta Lame**, have been rediscovered and, either developed by the council or claimed by Bologna's experimental youth, their intriguing architecture used to transform them into spectacular hybrids of nightclub and projection spaces. The old city docks and the tobacco factory, bakery and slaughterhouse around the **via del Porto** and **Giardino Cavaticcio** have been reincarnated as exciting arts centres under the umbrella name, La Manifattura delli Arti (the arts' factory). At a time when urban regeneration of industrial spaces*

*is all the rage, this area of Bologna is one of the most trendy, dynamic
and surprising in the city.*

▸▸ *See Sleeping p124, Eating and drinking p153, Bars and clubs p177*

◉ Sights

Palazzo Fava
via Manzoni 2. *Map 4, B3, p256*

This old family *casa signorile* (nobleman's house) is now occupied
by Bologna's prestigious Hotel Baglioni (p124). While you may not
be able to afford to stay here, it's possible to gain a free peek at the
beautiful frescoes by Annibale and Agostino Carracci on the first
floor, if you're discreet. In typical Italian style, Roman ruins have
recently been discovered under the breakfast room.

Museo Civico Medioevale e del Rinascimento
via Manzoni 4, **T** 051-203930. *Tue-Sat 0900-1830, Sun 1000-1830.
Closed Mon. €4, concessions €2. Map 4, B4, p256*

Located in the beautiful old noble 15th-century Palazzo Ghislardi
Fava, with its elegant entrance courtyard, this museum inspires
even those who are not immediately interested in its rich
collection of artefacts from the Renaissance and Middle Ages. Here,
against a wallpaper of paintings by the Carraccis and their pupils,
the enthusiast can admire myriad objects ranging from pieces of
armour and musical instruments to ceramics, tombs and busts of
popes and dignitaries, including one of Gregory XV by Bernini.

Chiesa della Madonna di Galliera
via Manzoni 5, **T** 051-230682. *0730-1200, 1600-1830.*
Map 4, A3, p256

Notable for its beautiful and delicate sandstone façade complete with figurines, this little 13th-century church, with 16th- and 17th-century additions and restorations, contains a number of important paintings in its many chapels, as well as a beautiful high altar by Francesco Bibiena.

Via Galliera
Map 2, G-E7, p253

The quiet via Galliera has always been one of Bologna's most aristocratic and well-to-do streets, lined with many fine *palazzi*, which, by their proximity to each other, illustrate very well how Bolognese architecture evolved over the centuries: 15th-century terracottas (numbers 13-15), 16th-century proportional harmony (numbers 3-5), and Baroque majesty (number 8). **Palazzo Calzolari** at number 14 houses many frescoes behind its terracotta façade; the 18th-century **Palazzo Montanari**, formerly a public building that's now sadly private, with its beautiful façade by Alfonso Torreggiani, is also home to many frescoes; and the **Casa delle Tuate** at number 6 borrowed its corner pillar from the destroyed Bentivoglio palace.

Stazione
piazza Medaglie d'Oro. *Map 2, D7, p253*

Although not architecturally significant in itself, Bologna's station nevertheless features as a milestone on the Italian public consciousness for the devastating terrorist bomb attack that claimed 88 victims there in August 1980. The bomb was planted by neo-fascist activists targeting Bologna as a renowned outpost of leftist thinking. Plaques on the outside of the station and on the main platform commemorate the dead and close scrutiny of the station building shows a seam where it has been rebuilt.

Chiesa dei Santi Gregorio e Siro
via Montegrappa 15. *Map 4, B1, p256*

On the corner of via Montegrappa and via Nazario Sauro, this
church used to be the home of the Ghisilieri family, their tower
having been neatly transformed into a campanile. The side chapels
inside contain famous paintings such as Annibale Carracci's
Baptism of Christ and two frescoes by Ludovico Carracci.

Mercato delle Erbe
via Ugo Bassi 2. *Map 4, B1, p256*

Bologna's covered market has occupied the elegant neo-classical
building between via Ugo Bassi and via Belvedere since 1910.
Inside row upon row of stalls are laden with fresh produce from
fruit and vegetables to dairy produce and meat – not the herbs
you'd expect from the name. In the annex is the **Mercato del
Pesce** (fish market), similarly well-stocked and more pungent.

Chiesa della Madonna del Colombano
entrance through the Casa dei Mutilato, via Parigi 1, **T** 051-232862.
0830-1130, 1530-1800. Visit to the upstairs oratory by request only.
Map 4, A3, p256

Long-covered by scaffolding, one of the real hidden treasures
of Bologna is the oratory on the first floor of this otherwise
unspectacular 16th-century church. It is arguably the most
concentrated symphony of artistic endeavour and the most beautiful
individual space in the whole city. The ground floor *Virgin and Child*
by Lippo di Dalmasio and other paintings by Antonio Carracci are a
prelude to the stunning upstairs oratory, which seems as if it were
almost a private chamber where Guido Reni, il Domenichino,
Lorenzo Garbieri and other pupils of the Carracci academy could
experiment with colours, forms, subjects and themes.

Teatro Arena del Sole

via dell'Indipendenza 44, **T** 051 2911910. *Mon 1530-1900, Tue-Sat 1100-1900. Map 2, G7, p253*

In contrast to Bologna's other main theatre, the Comunale, this 19th-century arena was conceived as a return to the Greco-Roman idea of a democratic theatre in the shape of a horseshoe. The theatre seats 900 people in its six tiers and was originally planned to host matinees.

Porta Galliera

Map 2, D8, p253

Reconstructed in 1661, this site marks the northern gate of the old city wall's 14th-century third circle.

Porto

via del Porto and around. *Map 2, E5-F6, p252*

In 2000, with increased public spending triggered by Bologna's nomination as a European City of Culture, work began on developing and revitalizing the area around via del Porto, which used to be the city's financial hub. This was the port area where the city's underground canals met the diverted Reno river and where the major commodities of the day – salt, marble, silk and hemp – were stored and traded. Only charitably could this area be called a true docklands in the sense of a maritime city (the river is a relative trickle) but its industrial warehouse architecture is nevertheless similar and, as is the fashion, is progressively being turned into a range of new cultural centres.

The redevelopment plan also forsees the continued restoration of the quays, brick steps, cast iron bollards and original paving of the port's heyday. The original port was dug in the area of Pora Lame, a commission given to the architect Jacopo Barozzi, otherwise known as *il Vignola*. A hole was made for the canal and up to 50 boats could be moored in the dock at one time. Still standing is the wharf, restructured in 1928 and covered by an arch near via Don Minzoni, inside which is an old 17th-century bridge. This area is being pedestrianized and, once it is lined with cafés and once the overgrown Cavaticcio gardens have been cleaned-up, it will, no doubt, make for a scenic, quasi 'left bank' atmosphere. The good record of the local government suggests the project will be a great success once it is finished.

La Manifattura delle Arti
Map 2, E4-F5, p256

'The Arts Factory' is the name give to the group of revitalised industrial building that are now exhibition areas and arts cinemas. The old **Tobacco Factory** on via Azzo Gardino has been transformed into a theatre, film library and centre for film studies. The Tobacco Factory building was once the 12th-century Benedictine monastery of Santa Maria Nova. Partially destroyed and renewed in the 16th century, it expanded to the nearby Cavaticcio gardens. In the 19th century, Napoleon closed the monastery and it was then that it took on its more secular role as a tobacco storage facility. The building was heavily bombed in World War II but still retains some of its Liberty (Italian art nouveau) features. The nearby **Slaughterhouse**, also on via Azzo Gardino, is the new home and projection room of the Lumière Cineclub.

The old **Bakery** on the corner of via Fratelli Rosselli and via Don Minzoni, a 1917 building that played an important role feeding the city in the First World War, is being redesigned to be, from 2006, the new home of the **Galleria d'Arte Moderna**, which is currently bursting at the seams in its space in the Fiera district (p87). The **Molino Tamburi**, a 18th-century paper mill alongside the Cavaticcio canal is due to open as a new university faculty of Communications as part of a design for the whole complex by architect Aldo Rossi, which foresees a raised walkway crossing the Cavaticcio gardens connecting the art gallery to the old dock.

The **Ex-Salara**, Bologna's salt warehouse, with its sloping floor designed to let the water drain away, has already been restored after it was abandoned in 1934 and buried in rubble. Downstairs in the basement is the new home of the ultra-trendy and very cool Cassero nightclub while upstairs is also to become an exhibition centre allied to the Modern Art gallery.

Exhibition Centre and around

*On the other side of the railway line begins the modern face of Bologna. In 1965 a **Zona Fiere** (Exhibition Centre) was built to cater for the increasing number of conventions, fairs and trade shows that were being hosted by the city. If Bologna has only recently become considered a tourist destination, it is because until now 80% of its visitors have been businessmen. The Quartiere Fieristico also has a park, a theatre and the Ducati factory.*

▸▸ *See Sleeping p127, Eating and drinking p156, Bars and clubs p179*

◉ Sights

Zona Fiere
piazza Costituzione. Information from: viale della Fiera 20,
T 051-282111, www.BolognaFiere.it   *Map 1, B12, p251*

Bologna's Exhibition Centre announces itself on the skyline with the towers designed by the Japanese architect, Kenzo Tange, in homage to the city's iconographic Due Torri. Le Corbusier bequeathed the area its L-shaped Esprit Nouveau pavilion, a legacy of the 1925 Paris Exhibition of the Decorative Arts, which was rebuilt in 1977. The original design for the whole area foresaw many more trees and green areas but these were never realized, leaving the complex rather bare and concrete. Aside from the halls, which house the

▶ Trade fairs

January *Arte Fiera* – Contemporary Art
February *Intimare* – Lingerie and swimwear
March *Saiedue* – Interior design; *Aipo* – fishing equipment
April Children's books and illustrators; *Cosmoprof* – perfumes and cosmetics
May *Lineapelle* – leather goods and fashion accessories
June *Intimare* – Lingerie and swimwear (again)
September *Sana* – healthfoods
October *Cersaie* – ceramics and bathroom design
November *Lineapelle* – leather and fashion goods
December *Motorshow* – cars, bikes and bicycles

stands and exhibitions of visiting shows, the complex incorporates the **Palazzo degli Affari e del Commercio** (the city's Chamber of Commerce) and also the **Galleria d'Arte Moderna** (Gallery of Modern Art, piazza della Costituzione 3, **T** 051-502859, www.galleria dartemoderna.bo.it, *Tue-Sun 1000-1800, closed Mon. €4, concession €2*). This museum houses a collection of over 2000 works of modern art, both Italian and international, including some important pieces by Carlo Carra, Giorgio de Chrico, Max Ernst and Jackson Pollock.

Parco Nord
Beyond the Fiera district.

Further along via Stalingrado (a road name that, like many others in this area, such as via Yuri Gagarin, emphasizes the city's leftist political stance) and just beyond the ring road, this park area is used for pop concerts, demonstrations and visiting circuses, and also has its own resident *Luna Park* where children and families can enjoy a fair experience of the real sort.

Bolognina
between via de' Carracci and via Francesco Barbieri.
Map 2, B6-A9, p252-p253

A human aspect of Bologna's modern face is represented by the small grid of multi-ethnic streets of *la Bolognina* (Little Bologna). These streets, full of the shops, cafés and restaurants of Bologna's immigrant communities from Africa, former Yugoslavia and the Orient add an interesting edge to Bolognese life.

Chiesa del Sacro Cuore
via Matteotti. *0800-1230 1500-1900. Map 2, C8, p253*

Further along the line of the railway, the eye is greeted by the extraordinary squat lump of this modern church, built at the turn of the 20th century and with not quite the same sense of proportion as the city's other places of worship – the nave seems too tall and fat for the cupola – but awe-inspiring in a different, more aggressive way.

Teatro Testoni
via Matteotti 16. **T** 051-377790. *Map 2, B8, p253*

Opposite the church, this theatre specializes in putting on plays and shows for and involving children.

Borgo Panigale
Northwest of the old centre, beyond the ringroad.

This is an industrial wasteland of little note other than that it is home to the Ducati factory, where the famous motorcycles, the equivalent of a Ferrari on two wheels, are still made. The **Museo Ducati**, (via C Ducati 3, **T** 051-6413111/6413259, *Mon-Fri 1100-1600, Sat 0930-1330 – visit by prior arrangement only*) retraces the history of the famous marque from its origins through to the present day. Many of the original prototypes and race-winning bikes that are now being replicated as production bikes as part of the Ducati renaissance are on display.

Hills to the south

*To the south of Bologna's old city walls, the countryside begins to bulge above the plain in a series of lush, undulating hills that rise to the lower Apennines beyond. In the immediate vicinity are three hills, Guardia, Osservanza and San Michele, which effectively belong to the city and which are linked to it, physically in the case of the extraordinary **Portico di San Luca**, by its spiritual and patrician past. Dotted in these hills are manicured and elegant summer residences such as the **villa Aldini** and **villa Spada**, beautiful monastical retreats like **San Michele in Bosco**, places of pilgrimage such as the **Basilica di San Luca** and natural havens of wild meadows in the **Parco di Villa Ghigi**. All are favourite weekend escapes for the Bolognese who come up to enjoy the peace and the spectacular panoramas over the city and the plain beyond. Apart from the unmissable walk up to the Basilica di San Luca, these places are best accessed by car. Ask at tourist information for local bus schedules.*

➤ *See Sleeping p127, Eating and drinking p156, Bars and clubs p179*

◉ Sights

★ Portico di San Luca

Follow the porticoes all the way from Porta Saragozza, in the southwest of the Centro Storico, up the hill to San Luca. *Map 1, F6-H1, p250*

Stretching for 3.6 km and encompassing 666 arches and 15 chapels en route, the construction of the portico which leads devotees and

Sunday strollers up the colle della Guardia from the Saragozza gate, is the longest continuous arcade in the world. An extraordinary feat of both architectural engineering and devotion, the building of the portico was simply intended to allow the people of Bologna to reach the object of their worship, the icon of San Luca held in the Santuario di San Luca at the hill's summit, without getting wet or sunburnt. This practical reason was no doubt mixed in with a sense of pride and Baroque extravagance and only conceivable by a city of considerable wealth. In a display of unity unusual among warring dynasties, each arch of the portico was financed by a combination of noble families, religious groups, merchants and artisans. Each group or family placed plaques and offerings opposite their arch in acts of worship and also to secure their own fame and immortality. Sadly most of these have now disappeared or been badly damaged, and the best example is probably the *Madonna and Child* (known as *la Madonna grassa*, the fat Madonna) by Andrea Ferri under the 170th arch. The portico was the design of the architect, Giovanni Monti. The first stone was laid in 1674 and the summit was reached in 1739. On the way up, Monti encountered several design conundrums, especially where the portico, having run along the plain, starts to lead uphill. This junction was secured by the construction of the Arco del Meloncello, an elaborate flurry of an arch designed by Carlo Francesco Dotti. At the steepest point of the incline, between the eighth and ninth chapels, a bridge was built to straddle the road.

Santuario della Madonna di San Luca

via di San Luca, **T** 051-6142339. *0700-1230 and 1430-1900. Free. For those not wishing to walk up the colonnade, Cosepuri runs a minibus from villa Spada to San Luca costing €1.50 each way with departures in the morning, around lunchtime and in the evening until 1900. To reach villa Spada, take bus 20 from via dell'Indipendenza. Map 1, H1, p250*

Bologna's arcades

Some enterprising person has calculated that there are 44 km of arcades in Bologna, including those leading up to San Luca but not including the modern arcades in rebuilt areas, such as via Marconi in the north west. The longest distance you can cover without emerging from underneath an arcade is the 8 km from the Chiesa degli Alemanni near porta Maggiore up to San Luca. Arcades are the city's leitmotif, loved by all for the changing perspectives and the tranquility they afford.

The first arcades are thought to have been built around the year 1000 to accommodate the city's expansion at the founding of the university and arrival of foreign students. Medieval additions sat precariously on top of houses with the support of wooden braces. Arcades were a practical solution for providing adequate support, increasing space above and providing shelter for pedestrians and merchants below. A law was passed making the minimum height seven feet so that people on horseback could pass under them. The symmetry of their design also fitted with the classical and humanist ideas of proportion and harmony that werebeing championed in the architecture of the time.

Sitting atop the Colle della Guardia hill at a height of 291 m this grandiose basilica is the home of the icon of San Luca, the religious saint of Bologna (as opposed to Petronius, the patron saint). Records tell of a religious community on the hill as far back as 1193 and an image of the Madonna has been exhibited in a small chapel there since that time. As with all the best icons, mystery and controversy surround the true origins and dating of the actual image that rests there to this day. One legend has it that it was discovered by a Greek monk in Constantinople, complete with a message that it should be installed on a hill somewhere called Monte della Guardia. When visiting the pope in Rome, he was informed of the hill outside Bologna and all agreed that the icon should be sent there. In actual fact, modern dating techniques show the icon to be 12th century; one theory is that the icon is a copy made by a Bolognese painter of a ninth- or tenth-century Byzantine-inspired work that probably passed through Bologna during the Crusades.

The basilica had a complete overhaul in the 18th century and, with the exception of some further alterations made between 1938 and 1950, the current building is the design of Carlo Dotti, started in 1723 and completed by his son, Gian Giacomo in 1775. From the outside, apart from the circular dome, the design looks more fit for a villa than a basilica, with its classical columns, arches and pediments and its Palladian harmonies. Cleverly though, the inside belies the exterior shape and does resemble the form of a church. The famous icon itself is kept in the company of numerous more beautiful paintings and frescoes. Especially worth seeking out are those by Donato Creti, the *Apparition of the Virgin to St Dominic* by Guido Reni and the *Apparition of Christ to the Virgin* by Guercino.

Ever since 1433 when increasing religious fervour elevated the Madonna di San Luca to the status of protector of the city, the people of Bologna have celebrated their icon in what has become the city's main unique festival. Every year in May, just before Ascension Day, a copy of the icon is brought down the portico in procession to be installed and exhibited for one week in the cathedral of San Pietro before being returned to its home on the hill (see Festivals, p191).

Villa Spada and Villa delle Rose

Villa Spada, via Casaglia 3. *Tue, Wed, Fri-Sun 0900-1300, Thu 0900-1300, 1500-1830, closed Mon.* Villa delle Rose, via Saragozza 228, **T** 051-436818. *Map 1, G4, p250*

Beyond the Porta Saragozza are many villas, mostly former summer residences of noble families. One of the most beautiful of these is the

Villa Spada, on the corner of via Casaglia. Situated by a stream in a refined Italian garden designed by Giovanni Martinietti, it is a postcard of neo-classical elegance. Built at the end of the 18th century, the building was originally owned by the Marquis Giacomo Zambeccari before, in 1831, becoming the headquarters of the invading Austrian army under Marshal Radetsky. It was here that the Italian patriot Ugo Bassi, after whom the city's main road is named, was tried and executed (actually at the Meloncello arch of the portico di San Luca). The villa then passed through many hands, including the Spada family, the tenor singer Antonio Poggi and, after it was damaged in the Second World War, became the property of the city.

Since 1966 it has housed the **Museo delle Tappezzerie** (**T** 051-6145512, *Tue-Sun 0900-1300, Thu also 1500-1800, entry €2.50, concessions €1.30*), a museum which retraces the fabrics and techniques of tapestry-making across various cultures, including over 6000 examples, some of which, such as the brocatelle which covered the Christian icons in the mosque of Hagia Sophia in Constantinople, are priceless pieces of religious history.

The 18th-century **Villa delle Rose**, on the opposing fork of via Saragozza, sits in a municipal park between an Italian garden and an English garden opened in 1930. The villa was originally built for the Cella family and is now used for occasional exhibitions as an extension of the Galleria di Arte Moderna (Gallery of Modern Art, p85). The parks and gardens of both villas are open all day.

San Girolamo della Certosa
via della Certosa. *0800-1700 in winter, 0700-1800 in summer.*
Map 1, E2-3, p250

Along via de Coubertin and via della Certosa is Bologna's main cemetery, resting place of the painter Giorgio Morandi (1890-1964), poet Giosue Carducci (1835-1907) and the composer, Ottorino Respighi (1879-1936). It is not, however, just a cemetery for the rich and famous; many more humble tombs are also to be found here, such as the first two to be laid in 1801 of Giuseppe Sarti, a baker, and Maddalena Brunini, a weaver. Enclosed within the cemetery walls is San Girolamo della Certosa, a 14th-century Gothic church with a portico and bell tower and, inside, a strange inverted design where a number of notable works of art can be viewed, such as the outsize paintings of *The Lord's Supper at the Pharisee's House* and *The Baptism of Christ*, by Giovanni and Elisabetta Sirani respectively.

Colle dell'Osservanza
South from piazza di Porta di San Mamolo but taking the southwesterly fork up via dell'Osservanza. *Map 1, H6, p250*

The Colle dell'Osservanza is named after the 'Observance' of the Franciscan Reforms that began in Bologna in the church of **San Paolo in Monte**. Located at the end of the road, this early 15th-century church commands beautiful views in all directions. These views are supposed to have been praised by Napoleon in 1805, whose eulogy fell on the ears of his ambassador, Antonio Aldini. Seeking to please the Emperor, Aldini got rid of the monks and, in 1881, commissioned a villa, the nearby neo-classical, temple-like **Villa Aldini** (via dell'Osservanza 35, **T** 051-580248, visit by arrangement only) to be given as a present. Sadly the Emperor never saw the completed villa as he was soon to meet his Waterloo. The villa is closed to the public except for occasional exhibitions.

Beneath the Osservanza hill on via San Mamolo is the **Parco di Villa Ghigi** (*daily 0900-1800*), accessible from the church of San Paolo in Monte through via di Gaibola. At 29 hectares, this is one of Bologna's largest parks, a beautiful rolling combination of rampant meadows and fields and cultivated, orderly vineyards. Within its dense vegetation are a great variety of towering trees, including many oaks, beeches and a yew, and in springtime the meadows are awash with tulips and many other flowers. The park is also a natural haven for a huge variety of animals. The austere **Villa Ghigi** (*closed to the public*), is a 19th-century make-over of an old 17th-century country house belonging to the Malvezzi family. Its owner until his death in 1970 was the zoologist Alessandro Ghigi, former rector of the university and a keen environmentalist. In 1960 he donated the grounds of the villa to the city as a park on the understanding that it would be kept for the protection of Bologna's indigenous wildlife.

San Michele in Bosco

piazza San Michele in Bosco, **T** 051-6266328. *0900-1200, 1600-1800 daily.* Map 3, H6, p244

South from piazza di Porta San Mamolo along via Codovilla is the hill of **San Michele in Bosco**. From its summit at 132 m the **Monastero degli Olivetani** dominates the city. Built in the 14th century by Olivetan monks on the site of a Gaulish temple, the monastery has since been used variously as a fort by the Bentivoglios against the Canetoli family, a barracks under Napoloeon and now as the seat of the Rizzoli Orthopaedic institute. The interior still houses many precious works of art, among which are the carved tombstone by Jacopo della Quercia to the right of the nave, a series of frescoes by Innocenzo da Imola in the Capitular Room, and most famously, the beautiful octagonal Carracci cloister, so-called after the well-known exquisite series of 37 frescoes depicting the *Lives of St Benedict, St Cecilia and St Valerian*, which the famous family of painters, ably aided by Guido Reni, worked on there. Some of the best views available of Bologna are to be enjoyed from the long esplanade that runs the length of the monastery, at 162 m, the largest covered space in Bologna.

● *From the large window overlooking the city within the monastery you can experience a strange telescopic effect whereby, if you are moving backwards, the Asinelli tower in the distance appears to grow bigger, not smaller.*

Giardini di Margherita
viale Gozzadini. *0600-midnight in summer, 0700-1800 Oct-Mar.*
Map 3, G/H10/11, p255

Just beyond the southern outer city wall of the Centro Storico,
between piazza di porta Santo Stefano and piazza di porta
Castiglione, lie the fine Margherita gardens, inaugurated in
1879 and named after the wife of King Umberto I. The gardens
were inspired by the Romantic design of the English parks of
the 19th century and were designed by Ernesto di Sambuy
from Piemonte.

At the centre is a lake complete with fountains reminiscent of
St James' and Regent's Park in London. Majestic cedars, pines and
chestnuts line the many paths and grassy areas that do their best
to replicate English lawns. A number of pavilions are dotted
around the park, vestiges of the Emilina Exhibition of 1888. From
the edge of the main lawn you can see an Etruscan sarcophagus,
part of a necropolis that was uncovered here when the gardens
were created.

This is Bologna's largest public park and, apart from being an
excellent place to stroll, sit, think or read, away from the bicycles
and shadowed stone arcades, it affords lovely vistas into the
rolling lower Apennines.

Museums and galleries

Listings

Biblioteca Universitaria Austere university library, home to over 900 thousand priceless tomes, p219.

Casa Carducci & Museo Civico del Risorgimento Last and favourite home of the poet Carducci and also a museum celebrating the creation of the Italian unified state in 1860, p72.

Civico Museo Bibliografico Musicale Important collection of original musical scores and manuscripts, p54.

Collezioni Comunali d'Arte Inside the citadel, various frescoes by famous Bolognese hands, p36.

Galleria d'Arte Moderna Minor abstract paintings and sculptures from the avant-garde to the present day, p85.

Museo Civico Archaeologico Locally excavated artefacts from Etruscan through to Roman times, p42.

Museo Civico Davia Bargellini Masterpieces from the 14th through to the 18th century, p71.

Museo Civico Medioevale Local Renaissance and Middle Ages artefacts in galleries decorated by the Carraccis, p81.

Museo del Patrimonio Industriale Bologna's role in industry from the 15th century and its history as a port (via della Beverara 123, T 051-6347770, *Tue-Sat 0900-1300, €4.13*).

Museo del Soldatino History and evolution of the toy soldier with thousands of models poised for battle (via Toscana 19, T 051-6236020, *Mon-Sat 0830-1230, Sun 0930-1230, free*).

Museo della Tappezzerie Fabrics and techniques of tapestry-making across various cultures, p93.

Museo di Anatomia Comparata History of the evolution of the human body, with tactile exhibits for the blind (via Selmi 3, T 051-2094243, *Mon-Fri 0830-1730, Sat and Sun 0900-1830*).

Museo di Antropologia Skulls and skeletons of Neolithic to 18th-century Italians (via Selmi 3, T 051-2094196, *open Mon-Fri 0830-1730, Sat and Sun 0900-1830*).

Listings

● **Museo di Mineralogia e Petrografia Luigi Bombucci**
Home to 50,000 pieces of planet Earth and elsewhere (piazza di
Porta S. Donato 1, T 051-2094926, Mon-Sat 0900-1300).

Museo di Paleontologia e Geologia Life on earth from
fossils and rocks to a giant dinosaur, p57.

Museo di Fisica Physics museum, arguably the home of
radio (via Irnerio 46, T 051-2091101).

Museo di San Domenico The history of the church of St
Dominic and the founding of the Dominican order, p70.

Museo di San Petronio Models for a bigger basilica, p33.

Museo di Santo Stefano Museum piecing together the
construction and expansion of the church complex, p68.

Museo di Zoologia One of the biggest zoological collections
in Italy (via Selmi 3, T 051-2094164, *Mon-Fri 0830-1730, Sat and
Sun 0900-1830*).

Museo Ducati The history of the famous motorbike, p88.

Museo Ebraico The history of Jews in Bologna (via Valdonica 1,
T 051-6569003, *Sun-Thu 1000-1800, Fri 1000-1600, €4.13, €2.07*).

Museo Morandi Largest collection of works by the
20th-century painter and celebrator of small things, p36.

Museo Storico dello Studio Exploring the history of study
(largo Trombetti 2, T 051-2099020).

Museo tattile di Pittura Antica e Moderna History of art in
Braille (via Castiglione 71, T 051-332090, *bookings only, free*).

Orto Botanico ed Erbario Botanical and herb gardens, p57.

Pinacoteca Nazionale Art by the Bolgnese masters, p58.

Planetario Basic introduction to the stars and man's obsession
for reading them (via Dante 5, T 051-348946, *groups only*).

Specola e Museo di Astronomia Filled with ancient and
bizarre star-gazing contraptions, p55.

Teatro Anatomico Totally wooden dissection theatre, p42.

Around Bologna

Apennine villages 101
The Apennines to the south have spa towns, castles and Etruscan remains.

Parma 104
Ham and cheese aside, Parma also has Romanesque architecture and great shopping.

Modena 106
Although smaller than Bologna, Modena appears more grandiose, its baroque architecture giving the true impression of a former city state.

Ferrara 109
A city of bikes and Renaissance art and planning, once hailed as the first modern city of Europe.

Imola 111
Despite Roman origins and beautiful churches, Imola is, more than anything, Formula One.

Ravenna 113
Briefly twilight capital of the Roman Empire and later lavished with Byzantine mosaics.

Rimini 113
You may simply want sea air, seafood and buzzing nightclubs, but Rimini can also offer culture.

Apennine villages

The hills behind Bologna are speckled with villages providing glimpses of rustic Italian life. They also provide the opportunity to savour the Apennine's rich flora and fauna and to take part in recreational activities, from trekking and climbing to cycling and skiing, or simply to relax at one of the area's spa towns. You will probably need your own transport to reach the deeper recesses of the region although buses do run to some of the bigger villages.

 Sights

Marzabotto
Museo Archaeologico Nazionale Pompeo Aria, via Porettana 13, T 051-932352. 0900-1200, 1500-1830, €2.50. Ruins 0800-1800. Buses at least once an hour from Bologna bus station, €10 return.

Ten or so kilometres southwest of Bologna, this village is famous for the considerable vestiges of the Etruscan town of Misa, dated to the sixth century BC and set in the beautiful wooded Monte Sole national park. Marzabotto also achieved notoriety as the place where 1800 partisan were massacred in 1944 during the last days of the Nazi occupation. Their names and faces are remembered on plaques on the side of the Palazzo Comunale in Bologna.

Montefiorino
Buses at least once an hour from Bologna bus station, €10 return.

Further west, atmospheric Montefiorino, with its steep approach and austere hilltop fort often surrounded in swirling mist, is another seat of partisan resistance in the summer of 1944.

▶ Park life

Around Bologna are numerous beautiful parks notable for their interesting geology and varied flora and fauna, including many birds of prey. They also contain biking trails and have bike hire facilities. Contact the tourist office for more information about the following parks: **Parco dell'Alto Apennino Modenese**, eagle country.

Parco del Delta del Po, 60 hectares of marshland and lagoons, perfect for birdwatching. **Parco dei Sassi di Rocca Malatina**, known for its sandstone needles and peregrine falcons. **Parco dello Stirone**, ambitiously likened to America's canyon country.

Castle Route

A car is necessary to do the whole route, though buses serve individual destinations. Ask tourist information for details.

The legacy of power and paranoia among warring factions in the area is visible in the many castles that dominate the hilltops. The following villages are connected by beautiful winding and tree-lined roads through the hills. Heading southwest of Bologna is **Vignola**, famous for its cherries and also for the **Rocca di Vignola** castle dating back to St Anselm. Beyond this is the 13th-century **Castello di Serravalle** before the route reaches the beautiful castle-town of **Monteveglio**, famous not only for its imposing fortress but also for the 11th-century abbey, **Abbazia di Santa Maria**, which acts as a focal point for great walks with stunning views over the countryside. At **Bazzano**, the fort is a piece of typically extravagant reconstruction work, commissioned by Giovanni II Bentivoglio in the 15th century on the remains of a 13th-century original. In the 18th century, the poet Ugo Foscolo was imprisoned in its tower. The castle now houses the **Museo Crespellani**, devoted to local history and archaeology. Bazzano is equally famous for its cherries and fine local wine. Further south still, **La Rocchetta Mattei** near Riola, is a castle of a different sort. Commissioned in 1850 by the eccentric homeopathic doctor Cesare Mattei, it is a fantastical fairytale hotchpotch of architectural influences from all cultures and eras, resulting in a Transylvanian rhapsody of kitsch. Nearby Riola is the home of an innovative church, the **Chiesa di Santa Maria l'Assunta** , a bold and unusual 1965 papal commission by the Finnish architect, Alvar Aalto.

Spa towns
Salsomaggiore Terme, Azienda Autunoma di Soggiorno e Cure, viale Romagnosi 4, **T** 0524-572100/578201. *Open all year.* **Porretta Terme**, via Roma 7, **T** 0534-22062. **Castel San Pietro**, viale Terme 1113, **T** 051-234475.

There are more than 20 thermal spa resorts in Emilia-Romagna, survivors of the 19th-century fashion for relaxing in sulphurous decadence. These are the perfect places to go in order to detox and hydro-massage away the extravagances of too much rich Bolognese food. The nearest to Bologna is at **Castel San Pietro,** only 23 km away but the most famous is **Salsomaggiore Terme**, 32 km west of Parma. Nowadays it's a bustling resort of 41 hotels, dedicated to the twin Italian religions of health and beauty, but it has magnificent art deco architecture and still retains a belle epoque *Death In Venice* atmosphere. Nearby is the **Terme Felsinee** complex, part of the **Porretta Terme**. Porretta is the place to come for a quieter experience. The spa is located in prime Morandi country (you will pass through the Cezanne-like hills of Grizzana Morandi on the way), 60 km south of Bologna at an altitude of 349 m.

Parma

The attributes of Parma read like a mouthwatering shopping list from the local delicatessen: Parma ham, Parmesan cheese and the Barilla empire that makes half the pasta in Italy. It's a sensuous enclave of affluence, elegance, sophistication, fine opera and gourmet food, whose people are convinced that their city is the centre of the universe. Retaining the snobbery which came with French rule under Napoleon's wife, Maria Luigia, they regard their town as 'la petite capitale' of Italy.

Aside from strolling and window-shopping through the sunny, yellow-tinged aristocratic streets of the Farnese dynasty that ruled here from the mid-16th to the mid-18th century, Parma has a number of imperatives on the sights shopping list.

▸▸ *See Sleeping p129, Eating and drinking p161*

◉ Sights

Duomo
piazza Duomo. *Daily 0900-1200, 1500-1900.*

Parma's cathedral is a beautifully delicate wonder of 11th-century Romanesque architecture, with three rows of loggias and containing famous frescoes and friezes by the artists Correggio (the *Assumption* in the central cupola) and his pupil, Parmigianino, in the southern transept. The beautiful octagonal **baptistery** (hours as above), built in red Veronese marble, with turrets, elaborate portals and a surrounding frieze, is the masterwork of the architect, Benedetto Antelami, and was completed in 1196.

Chiesa di San Giovanni Evangelista
piazza Duomo. *Daily 0600-1200 , 1530-2000.*

To the east of the Duomo, this church contains famous frescoes by Correggio of the *Vision of St John*.

> **Parmesan cheese**

If you want to see how its made, visit one of the main dairies, the **Caseificio Consorzio Produttori Latte**. Tours can be arranged by **Consorzio del Formaggio Parmigiano Reggiano**, T 0521-292700. You'll meet the Master Cheesemaker, taste all sorts of different types of parmesan (and parma ham), washed down with some local wine. Be prepared for an early start. If you can't spare the time for the tour, the Caseificio, in Baganzolino, offers great truckles of parmesan at reduced prices.

Camera di San Paolo
off via Melloni.

The back room of this former convent is famous for the daring and sensuous collection of frescoes commissioned by the abbess Giovanna and painted in 1518 by Correggio (aka Antonio Allegri). They are widely considered to be among his most significant work.

Palazzo della Pilotta
piazza Pilotta.

Unmissable by its size, this former palace of the Farnese dynasty is now the home to a complex of museums, the most important of which is the city's art gallery, the **Pinacoteca** (*Tue-Sat 0900-1400, Sun 0900-1300, €5*), where many spectacular works by Correggio and Parmigianino are on display, alongside others by the Carraccis, Tiepolo, Canaletto and Leonardo da Vinci. Also within the Palazzo della Pilotta is the **Teatro Farnese** (*entry included on gallery ticket*), entirely rebuilt in wood as it was before being bombed in 1944.

Across the river Parma stands the 16th-century **Palazzo Ducale**, former residence of Ottaviano Farnese, among an enormous and relaxing park of 18th-century gardens.

Casa Toscanini

borgo R Tanzi. *Tue and Sat 1000-1300, 1500-1800, Wed-Fri, 1000-1300. Free.*

The musician and conductor, Arturo Toscanini, was born in this house on 25th March,1867. He attended Parma's Royal School of Music at the age of nine and graduated at 18. Parma was also the home of the musicians and composers, Verdi and Paganini.

Teatro Regio

via Garibaldi 16a, **T** 0521-218685/218678.

The musical tradition of the city is characterized by the opera house which attracts exacting audiences not afraid to boo during bad performances and organize *claques* (fan clubs) in support of favourites – in tune with opera's origins.

Modena

*Situated 41 km northwest along the via Emilia, Modena has always been Bologna's closest and fiercest rival. It all apparently started with a stolen wooden bucket. The Modenese were Ghibelline supporters of the Emperor Frederick II and were furious when their Guelph neighbours kidnapped his son, Re Enzo. They raided Bologna and came away with the secchia rapita (stolen bucket), which thereafter became a symbol of the cities' rivalry, immortalized in a satirical poem by Alessandro Tassoni. Even today the cities mockingly squabble over supremacy in measurements of gastronomy and fast cars. The majestic **Duomo** and the impenetrable, huge bulk of the **Palazzo Ducale** dominate the city but also make it feel colder and more clinical, lacking the vibrancy and* *spontaneity of Emilia's capital. This is reflected in its citizens who come across as more 'comodo' (literally 'comfortable' but meaning a cross between complacent and conceited). That said, the concentric medieval centre, a tight network of labyrinthine streets built around a central square, is a pleasure to wander around and get lost in.*

▸▸ *See Sleeping p129, Eating and drinking p161, Bars and clubs p182*

◉ Sights

Duomo

corso Duomo 6, **T** 059-223474. *Mon-Sat 1030-1200, 1530-1730.*

Dominating the piazza Grande is the 12th-century cathedral to the city's patron saint, San Geminiano, recognized as one of the finest examples of Romanesque architecture in Italy. The western façade is famous for its graceful columns and two majestic lions that support the central portal. This is surrounded by bas reliefs depicting scenes from *Genesis* and from the Arthurian cycle, the work of the sculptor Wiligelmo completed around 1100. The beautiful polychrome stained-glass windows inside, in particular *The Last Supper*, are the work of Giovanni da Modena, completed around 1450. The cathedral's other salient feature is its 88-m high leaning bell-tower, nicknamed *La Torre Ghirlandia* (the garland tower). Half Gothic and half Romanesque, it used to contain the offending wooden bucket. The cathedral was named a UNESCO World Heritage site in 1997.

Palazzo Ducale

piazza Roma. *Closed to the public.*

Occupying the entire northeastern flank of piazza Roma, you will not be able to miss the vast 15th-century palace that was the former court of the Este dynasty who ruled Ferrara (see p110) during the Guelph and Ghibelline feuds of the 13th-16th centuries but subsequently decamped and brought affluence to Modena following defeat by Cesare Este at the hands of the Pope in 1598. This palace was the family's court and an extravagant display of fading might in its twilight years. Rather blunt and fortress-like in aspect, it is now a military academy.

Palazzo dei Musei

piazzale Sant'Agostino 337, **T** 059-222145. *Tue, Fri, Sat 0900-1900, Wed, Thu 0900-1400, Sun 0900-1300, €4.*

The Palazzo dei Musei is a complex housing the city's main museums and galleries. On the first floor is the **Biblioteca Estense**, the collected correspondence of a despotic family dynasty with its rival emperors and popes. It is also the home of the famous **Bibbio Borso**, the lavishly illustrated and priceless bible of Borso d'Este. On the second floor is the **Museo d'Arte Medievale e Moderne e Etnologie**, a specialist collection of archaeological relics and artifacts. The most important floor is at the top, where the fabulous art collection of the Este family is hung in the **Galleria Estense**, combing paintings from the early Renaissance and masterpieces by the Carraccis, Guercino and Guido Reni, as well as sculptures by Niccolo dell'Arca. There is also a bust of Francesco d'Este by Bernini and Venetian canvasses by Tintoretto and Veronese.

Also worthy of architectural note are the clock tower of the **Palazzo Comunale** and the pretty churches of **San Francesco** (13th-century) and **San Pietro** (14th-century).

Galleria Ferrari

via Dino Ferrari 43, Galleria Ferrari **T** 0536 949714. Galleria@ Ferrari.it *Daily except Mon, from 0930-1230 and 1500-1800, €10, concessions €6. Bus 2 from Modena (every half hour).*

Visitors in search of something a little more contemporary will

know that Modena was the birthplace of Enzo Ferrari, founder of the famous 'prancing horse' stable of red racing cars. He founded the factory at nearby **Maranello**, south of Modena and *tifosi* (fans) can retrace the glory years and see many classic models old and new on display at the Galleria museum.

Ferrara

Ferrara owes its Imperial aspect to the powerful Este dynasty who made the city their stronghold from the 13th to 16th centuries, elevating it from inauspicious beginnings in the middle of a fly-ridden Po delta swamp, and keeping the major artists of the day, such as Pisanello, Mantegna and Jacopo Bellini as well as poets such a Ludovico Ariosto, in work with numerous extravagant commissions. Ferrara is also the Italian capital of bikes. Locals trundle around lazily on them, lending the city an air of gentle provinciality that alleviates the domineering mortar of powers past. The centre of palace-lined arcaded streets, encircled by 9 km of ancient city wall, was declared a UNESCO World Heritage sight in 1995.

▸▸ *See Sleeping p130, Eating and drinking p162*

◉ Sights

Castello Estense
piazza Castello, **T** 053-22992733. *Tue-Sun, 0930-1730, €5*

Dominating the main square is the brutal, prison-like castle, surrounded by a moat, the former seat of the Este family. Behind its walls lived the court, which starred, among others, the poets Ariosto and Tasso. Inevitably more elegant inside than its exterior image of power was meant to show, much of the building is now used for offices and is inaccessible. The *saletta* and *salone dei giochi* (games room), decorated by Sebastiano Filippi, contain colourful and energetic images of sports. The castle was begun at the end of the 14th century, commissioned by Nicolo II d'Este.

> ### The Este dynasty

The beginning of the Este family's dominance began in 1264 with Obizzo II, who with the support of Venice was summoned to reinforce the Guelph sympathizers in Ferrara. On his arrival he would have found a rather dull town. However, he was to be the first of 15 Este princes to laud it over the local populace and to bring great wealth, art and prosperity to Ferrara. When the dynasty fell in 1598, under Cesare d'Este, the family moved to Modena and took much of their prosperity with them.

Duomo
piazza Trento e Trieste. *Tue-Sat 0830-1200, 1500-1830, Sun, 1000-1200, 1600-1800.*

Like that of Modena, Ferrara's cathedral is a mixture of the Gothic and Romanesque. Built between the 12th and 14th centuries, it features work on the central portal of its façade by the same architect, Wiligelmo. Inside it is more like an opulent palace and the **museum** (**T** 053-2207449, *Tue-Sat 1000-1200, 1600-1800, free/donation*) upstairs contains a collection of important bas-reliefs and a *Madonna* by Jacopo della Quercia.

Palazzo Schifanoia
via Scandiana 23. *0900-1900 daily, €4.*

Roughly translated as 'Palace for Dispelling Boredom' this palazzo was certainly built for the amusement of the Este family. They commissioned Cosimo Tura, head of the Ferrara school of painting, to paint delightful escapist frescoes of the four seasons on the walls of the *salone dei mesi* (room of months), each linked with signs of the zodiac and everyday scenes of the court. Remarkably this cycle was not discovered until 1820, having been covered up by the papacy who took control of the city in 1598. The palazzo also houses the city's museum of local history and archaeology.

Palazzo dei Diamanti
corso Ercole d'Este 21, **T** 053-2205844. *Tue-Sat 0900-1400, Sun 0900-1300, €4.*

Further north, in the grand part of the city planned by Ercole I d'Este, is the 15th-century Palazzo dei Diamanti, probably named after Ercole whose nature was said to be as cold as a diamond. Diamond-shapes also feature in the nail-headed marble bossages on the façade. The palazzo houses a number of the city's museums, most notably, on the first floor, the city's main art gallery, **La Pinacoteca Nazionale** (*Tue-Sat 0900-1400, Sun 0900-1300, E3,50*) where works by Cosimo Tura and other interpreters of the Ferrara school are on display. Aside from the usual local history museums, there is also a museum to the work of the Ferrara-born film director Michelangelo Antonioni, of *Blow-Up* fame.

Imola

*Imola has a Roman forum, many beautiful churches and a couple of museums, but you could be forgiven for making the only object of your visit here a trip to the world-famous **Autodromo Dino Ferrari**. Built in 1950 on the site of a Roman amphitheatre that would have witnessed many chariot races, the circuit hosts many racing events and also concerts throughout the year, but most importantly the **San Marino Grand Prix**. Imola is otherwise a pleasant, quiet place to wander around, with an intact old centre and a grid of ancient, narrow pedestrian streets, opening into classic Italian piazzas, complete with attendant bars, cafés and restaurants.*

▸▸ *See Sleeping p130, Eating and drinking p162*

Sights

Autodromo Dino Ferrari

information/tickets: piazzale da Vinci 1, Imola, **T** 0542 34116,
www.autodromoimola.com *Fri-Sun 0800-1900. Taxi **T** 0542 28122
from the stand by Imola railway station or piazza Matteotti.*

For the Grand Prix, the passionate *tifosi* (fans) of the home Ferrari
team literally paint the town red (p205). Situated about 30 km
from Bologna, the circuit is well-signposted both from the A14
motorway and the centre of Imola.

Rocca Sforzesca

piazzale Giovanni delle Bande Nere, **T** 054-223472. *May-Sep,
Sat-Sun 0900-1200, 1500-1900, entry €2.50.*

The size and power of this fortress, with its four squat towers like
castles from a chess set, seems incongruous in the context of
modern-day Imola but in medieval times it was the residence of
the powerful Sforza family. It was built between the mid-13th and
15th centuries, designed by Gian Galeazzo Visconti. Its purpose
now is considerably more humble as a museum of armoury and
medieval ceramics and the setting for occasional summer concerts.

Zoo Acquario

via Aspramonte, **T** 0542-24180. *Tue-Sat, 0900-1200, 1530-900, Sun
0930-1200, 1530-1900.*

Visitors looking for a day out with kids might be interested in
heading for the tropical and marine fish and animals on display here.

Ravenna

Ravenna was coveted by invading forces, so much so that the Byzantines, arriving after the Goths, endowed it with mosaics, which are generally considered to be the finest examples of Byzantine art existing anywhere in the world. The mosaics are still remarkably intact despite bombs and 20th-century industrial ravishment.

Sights

Mosaics

The mosaics are scattered in various locations around town, in the **Museo Arcivescovile** and **Battistero** on piazza Arcivescovile (*both open daily from 0900-1900*, €1.80) and in the **Basilica di Sant'Apollinaire Nuovo** on via di Roma. By far the most famous and richest concentration of mosaics, however, is to be found around the **Basilica di San Vitale** (*via Fiandrini, T 054-434266, Jun-Oct 0900-1900*), itself a wonder of geometric Byzantine design, built in 548 and the model for the Hagia Sofia in Istanbul. Inside the basilica and across the lawn in the **Mausoleo di Galla Placidia** is a remarkable mind bogglingly intricate tapestry of mosaics.

Rimini

*Now regarded as the Italian equivalent of Ibiza, Rimini was once an important Adriatic port and has some fascinating Roman remains. The **Arco d'Augusto**, dated to 27 BC, is one of the oldest surviving Roman arches in Italy. Older still is the five-arched bridge of **Ponte di Tiberio**, built in 22 BC out of white Istrian stone. The town was also the birthplace and psychological inspiration of the film director Federico Fellini, whose film* Amarcord *records his childhood here.*

▶▶ *See Sleeping p130, Eating and drinking p163, Bars and clubs p182*

Sights

Tempio Malatestiano
piazza San Francesco. *Tue-Sat 0830-1230, 1700-1900, Sun 1600-1900. €4.*

It was not really until the 15th century that Rimini reached the apogee of its power under the extraordinary prince-inventor-scientist-strategist-humanist, Sigismondo Malatesta. It is to him and his love for his third wife, Isotta degli Atti, that the city owes the magnificent and eclectic pagan Tempio Malatestiano. Originally a Gothic church to St Francis, Malatesta had its façade transformed by Alberti to reflect the motifs of the Arco d'Augusto. The pagan theme continues inside with angels, cupids, roses and elephants by Agostino di Duccio adorning the side chapels. The crucifix in the chapel of Isotta has been attributed to Giotto and the walls of the Reliquary Chapel are adorned by a magnificent and indulgent fresco of *Sigismondo praying at the Feet of St Sigsmondo* painted in 1451 by Piero della Francesca.

Beaches
Rimini's beaches are signposted from the bus and train stations.

Riccione and Cattolica are the two main beach resorts but the Italian concept of a beach is unlikely to coincide with that of most visitors. As elsewhere in Italy, the whole coast has been carved up into *bagni*, private beaches the size of postage stamps which attract varying degrees of snobbery according, it would seem, to the colour of the parasols and deckchairs. There are virtually no public places to enjoy. You will be sandwiched between other towels, quickly have sand kicked in your face by a nearby game of beach tennis, or be pestered by one of a sweltering army of watch/sponge/glasses/you-name-it vendors. That said, the views of pectorally perfect men and glossy gilded lilies are fantastic.

Sleeping

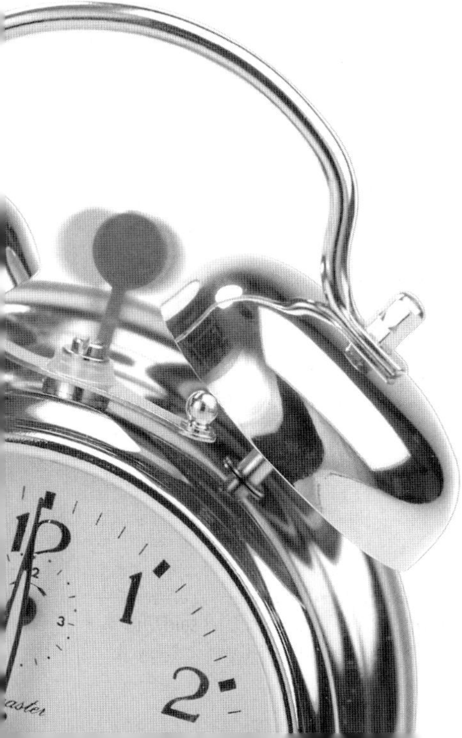

Due to the city's prominence as a centre for business, Bologna is well-stocked with hotels, although those outside the Centro Storico have been conceived for the business traveller and are blandly decorated. During trade fairs, capacity is quickly exhausted, so book well in advance. Although rooms in central hotels are rarely spacious, due to their medieval proportions, every effort should be made to stay in the old centre, since this area is the focus for both sights and atmosphere. If you are looking for a view, ask for a room high up to allow for the porticoes and narrow streets. These are also quieter, although, for absolute insulation from mopeds, you will need to forgo the view for a room over a courtyard. With one or two exceptions (see www.bolognarthotels.it), hip and contemporary design hasn't really hit Italy's hotels. Most are old and architecturally interesting buildings, decorated with 1970s interiors and an assortment of dreary furniture. Budget options are improving, however, as the concept of 'bed and breakfast' catches on; the tourist office's website, www.bolognaturismo.it, has a complete listing.

€ **Sleeping codes**

Price

LL	€300 and over	C	€75-99
L	€250-299	D	€50-74
AL	€200-249	E	€35-49
A	€150-199	F	€25-34
B	€100-149	G	€24 and under

Prices are for a double room in high season.

Most rooms have en-suite bathrooms although dimensions often dictate that they will have a shower rather than a bath. Few hotels have single rooms and solo travellers will usually have to pay a supplement. Payment by card is generally accepted in the bigger hotels but others will prefer or, in some cases, only accept cash. A hotel tax of 10% is usually included in the bill, as is breakfast. However, you will have a more authentically Italian experience if you start the day with a coffee and pastry at one the city's multitude of bars.

Outside the city, Modena's narrow medieval streets offer a number of pleasing hotels for a stopover but booking ahead is essential and there are few budget options. In Rimini some might argue that sleeping is for the daytime on the beach but there are some alternatives. Imola's hotels are unspectacular and the city might be better done as a day-trip from Bologna.

Centre: piazza Maggiore and around

AL Cappello Rosso, via De' Fusari 9, **T** 051-261891, **F** 051-227179, www.alcappellorosso.it *One block west of via D'Azeglio, near piazza Maggiore. Map 4, E2, p 256* Over 600 years old, this hotel reputedly lodged the builders of the Basilica San Petronio as it was the only place with hot water. The 35 rooms are very comfortable, if a little dark. The attic suite on the fourth floor is especially cosy. The hotel has disabled facilities as well as parking for a supplement.

AL Commercianti, via de' Pignattari,11, **T** 051-7457511, **F** 051-7457522, www.bolognarthotels.it *Just south of piazza Maggiore. Map 4, E3, p256* Next to the basilica of San Petronio, ask for a room on 3rd floor overlooking the church, nearly within touching distance. Suite 319 is especially well-decorated. This hotel used to be part of the town hall and still retains some original woodwork in its structure. Recently restored it has a garage and modern facilities.

A Orologio, via IV Novembre, 10, **T** 051-7547411, **F** 051-7457422, www.bolognarthotels.it *A stone's throw from the southwest corner of piazza Maggiore. Map 4, D2, p256* On a pedestrian street with 32 rooms, some with fine views over the palazzo comunale, a garage and a tearoom. The eponymous clock is on the façade (it doesn't strike at night). The walls have accidentally retro fabric designs.

B Apollo, via Drapperie 5, **T** 051-237904. *Between piazza Maggiore and the two towers. Map 4, D4, p256* Clean and spacious in the atmospheric alleyways of the quadrilatero.

C Garisenda, via Rizzoli 9, Galleria del Leone 1, **T** 051-224369, **F** 051-221007. *On the edge of piazza di Porta Ravegnana, very near the two towers. Map 4, D5, p256* Clean and friendly, run by an old couple. Rooms are on the third floor of an old palazzo and so command good views of the two towers. Best to book.

D Centrale, via della Zecca, 2, **T** 051-225114, **F** 051-223899/ 051-235162. *Between via Ugo Bassi and piazza Roosevelt. Map 4, E3, p256* This centrally located and unpretentious hotel in an old noble's house offers spacious and tastefully decorated rooms on the 3rd floor, many of which have good views to the Due Torri and over the city rooftops. The reception, bar area and salon are impeccably maintained by the owner, Werther Guizzardi.

D Galileo, piazza Galileo 3, **T/F** 051-237452, www.galileobed andbreakfast.com *South of via IV Novembre. Map 4, E2, p256* Ten economical bedrooms, bang in the centre.

Northeast: the university quarter

L San Donato, via Zamboni 16, **T** 051-235395, **F** 051-230547, www.hotelsandonato.it *Northeast from piazza di Ravegna, opposite the Palazzo Malvezzi de' Medici. Map 4, C7, p256* In a plum location under the two towers and on the edge of the university quarter. Part of the Best Western group this hotel escapes feeling like a chain hotel due to its individual period furnishings and its personal service. A terrace bar overlooking rooftops is a perfect place for an evening campari and the ice-cream stand opposite the entrance is a creamy bonus.

AL Corona d'Oro, via Oberdan 12, **T** 051-7457611, **F** 051-7457622, www.bolognarthotels.it *Just north of via Rizzoli. Map 4, C5, p256* The 15th-century Azzoguidi palazzo, a hotel since the early 1800s, still retains much of its antique charm despite being recently renovated. Part of it is supported on wooden porticoes, the entrance is an elegant Venetian-style belle époque veranda and some rooms have wonderful painted wood ceilings. All 35 rooms have en-suite shower facilites. There is a breakfast room but no restaurant. Bicycles, guided tours, theatre tickets, discounts at restaurants and cookery courses all available on request. Classical music concerts are sometimes organized in the mornings. Garage at extra cost.

AL Tre Vecchi, via dell'Indipendenza 47, **T** 051-231991, **F** 051-224143, www.zanhotel.it/trevecchi *Just south of piazza VIII Agosto. Map 2, G7, p253* An elegant hotel with a classic tasteful turn-of-the-century decor in pale green shades. 96 airy and well-appointed rooms with all modern comforts.

B Cavour, via Goito 4, **T** 051-228111, **F** 051-222978. *Off via dell' Independenza north of the Cattedrale di San Pietro. Map 4, A4, p256* Very central and comfortable if unspectacular. Rooms with en suite bathrooms and a/c.

B Donatello, via dell'Indipendenza 65, **T** 051-248174, **F** 051-248174, www.hoteldonatello.com *Just to the west of piazza VIII Agostso. Map 2, F7, p253* Bland but comfortable rooms on this main street. Avoid the rooms at the front which can be noisy.

C Holiday, via Bertiera 13, **T** 051-235326, **F** 051-235326, www.hotelholiday-bo.com *Off via dell' Independenza between piazza Otto Agosto and the Cattedrale di San Pietro. Map 2, G7, p253* This functional and well thought out establishment alternates opening weeks with its partner hotel, the University (see below) in July and August. Studios and kitchens are available for longer visits. Single rooms have large beds. Bicycles for hire.

C Paradise, via Cattani 7, **T** 051-231792, **F** 051-234591, www.informatutto.it/hotelparadise.net *Off via dell' Independenza between piazza Otto Agosto and the Cattedrale di San Pietro. Map 2, H8, p253* This ambitiously named hotel has 18 rooms, the top ones with good views and architectural character. Following a refit, all are brightly decorated. Situated among some of Bologna's fascinating side-streets, near canals and arcaded streets, Monica and Marisa will make you feel at home. Bike hire possible.

C **Regina**, via dell'Independenza 51, **T** 051-248878, **F** 051-247986. *On the southwest corner of piazza Otto Agosto. Map 2, G7, p253* Opposite the Arena del Sole theatre and next to the market are 61 rooms decorated in a classic, English style, the better ones overlook the rear of the hotel.

C **University**, via Mentana 7, **T** 051-229713, **F** 051-229713, info@hotel-university.com *Off via delle Moline, just south of Palazzo Bentivoglio. Map 4, A6, p256* The University hotel has unspectacular rooms but it is near the municipal theatre, making it a good choice for music lovers. Alternate weeks of closure during July and August with the Holiday hotel (see above).

D **Giardinetto**, via Massarenti 76, **T** 051-342793, **F** 051-342816, info@hotelgiardinetto-bo.com *East of piazza di Porta San Vitale. Map 3, B12, p255* 24 comfortable and spacious rooms just outside the city walls, adjacent to the university clinic and Porta San Vitale.

D **Orsola**, via Palmieri 25, **T** 051-302997, **F** 051-302997, rolima.fe@libero.it *East of piazza di S Vitale. Map 1, F11, p251* Unsophisticated rooms within staggering distance of student bars.

D **Perla**, via San Vitale 77/2, **T** 051-224579. *Just northwest of piazza Aldrovandi. Map 3, A11, p255* Literally meaning 'pearl' this is hardly a gem. Very much like a youth hostel, with no charm and no English, it is at least clean and cheap. Separate bathrooms. Rooms have a safe, toilet and basin.

D **Rossini**, via Bibbiena 11 , **T** 051-237 716, **F** 051-268035. *Just southeast of piazza G Verdi. Map 3, A10, p255* A friendly choice in prime studentland.

Sleeping

D San Giorgio, via Moline 17, **T** 051-248659, **F** 051-250556, info@sangiorgiohotel.it *North of the Basilica di S Martino. Map 2, G8, p253* Reliable choice with a good atmosphere.

D San Vitale, via San Vitale 94, **T** 051-225966, **F** 051-239396. *Opposite via dell' Unione. Map 3, B11, p255* Under porticoes but the beauty finishes there. Simple, big, quiet rooms, sunny interior garden, basic MFI furniture.

E BBA Bologna, via Cairoli 3, **T/F** 051-4210897, takakina @hotmail.com Comfortable bed and breakfast, close to the station and the central sights. Multilingual staff. Some rooms are en suite – a rarity in Italy, especially at this end of the cost spectrum.

E Rimondi Monica, via Mascarella 31, **T/F** 051-245924. *Between via delle Belle Arti and via Irnerio. Map 2, G10, p253* Bed and breakfast – one single room with a bathroom on the third floor, three bedrooms with bathroom and kitchen on the ground floor.

Southeast: around Santo Stefano

B Hotel Touring, via Mattuiani 1, **T** 051-584305, **F** 051-334763, www.hoteltouring.it *Just off piazza dei Tribunali. Map 3, D7, p255* Refurbished and well-equipped while managing to retain elegance and harmonious decor with mellow colours and touches of stucco. Non-smoking rooms, garage, solarium. Large panoramic roof terrace with a view of the Bologna hills. Bicycles available.

C Blumen, via Mazzini 45, **T** 051-344672, **F** 051-345439, hotelblumen@tin.it *Near piazza di Porta Maggiore. Map 1, G11, p251* Located in a completely restored old building just outside the city walls, this hotel has spacious rooms with parquet floors and sparse decoration. Private parking.

C Pedrini, strada Maggiore 79, **T** 051-3400081, **F** 051-341436. *Near the corner of strada Maggiore and via della Fondazza. Map 3, C12, p255* Central accommodation on the old via Emilia. Comfortable modern rooms and facilities including interior parking.

C Porta San Mamolo, via del Falcone 6/8, **T** 051-583056, **F** 051-331739, www.hotel-portasanmamolo.it *Between via Paglietta and via Miramonte Ruini. Map 3, E6, p254* A small romantic hotel in a formerly seedy district of the historic centre, refurbished with all comforts, inside garden and a/c.

E Bonzagni, via Schiassi 52, **T/F** 051-346905. *Map1, F12, p251* Bed and breakfast in a family villa. Double rooms with separate bathroom and private living room.

Southwest: around via del Pratello

AL Novecento, piazza Galileo 4, **T** 051-7547311, **F** 051-7547322, www.bolognarthotels.it *Map 4, D2, p256* The latest addition to Bologna's growing list of boutique hotels, the Novecento is the only upscale accommodation in the southwest centre of Bologna. The decor harks back to the clean, angular lines of the 1930s – all wood, leather and discreet lighting. All mod-cons plus private parking and free bikes for guests. With only 25 rooms, this is a peaceful, luxurious and uniquely hip address in the medieval city.

B Re Enzo, via Santa Croce 26, **T** 051-523322, **F** 051-554035. *Western edge of the Centro Storico between via del Pratello and via San Felice. Map 2, H2, p252* Small and standard but relatively charming Best Western hotel with American bar. Modern and comfortable rooms. Garage parking with supplement.

C Miramonte, via Miramonte 11, **T**3395697513 (mob), www.miramonte-bologna.it *Just south of via Solferino.* *Map3, E6, p254* Central and cheap option near the impressive law courts.

D Panorama, via Livraghi 1, **T** 051-221802, **F** 051-266360. South off via Ugo Bassi. *Map 4, C1, p256* Situated on the 4th floor of an elegant building, this small and welcoming family hotel offers good value for money. Rooms range from doubles to four-bed rooms but none is en-suite. The shared bathrooms down the corridor are kept very clean.

E Senzanome, via Senzanome 14, **T/F** 051-6449245, www.users @iol.it/coruzzi/B&B *North of via Saragozza between via del Fossato and via Nosadella.* *Map 3, C4, p254* The hotel with no name. First floor accommodation, 10 minutes from piazza Maggiore. One double with private bathroom and turn-of-the-century furniture.

Northwest: around via Galliera

LL Baglioni, via dell'Indipendenza 8, **T** 051-225 445, **F** 051-234 840, ghb.bologna@baglioni-palacehotels.it *At the southern end of via dell'Independenza.* *Map 4, B3, p256* On the busy main drag up to piazza Maggiore, to judge by the bill this is Bologna's only luxury address. The hotel, however, is beginning to look a little tired, especially in the 125 rooms beyond the foyer. That said, it is in a fine 16th-century building with a grand entrance under the porticoes complete with gloved and uniformed porters. There are frescoes by the Caracci brothers in the foyer and hallways, a health suite, and if you don't feel like venturing out for supper there is the renowned Caracci restaurant (with more frescoes by the masters).

A Starhotel Excelsior, viale Pietramellara 51, **T** 051-246178, **F** 051-249448, www.starhotels.com *Opposite the station just off piazza delle Medaglie d'oro.* *Map 2, D6, p252*

Modern but unspectacular 'luxury' hotel with all business facilites and mod cons. The back rooms overlook a garden. It's overtly designed for business travellers, although the minimalist chic foyer and bar area, a homage to Philip Stark, also manages to attract an evening crowd.

A **Internazionale**, via dell'Indipendenza 60, **T** 051-245544, **F** 051-249544, www.monrifhotels.it *On the corner of via dei Mille. Map 2, F7, p253* Comfortable and popular with business travellers. 120 elegant and recently refurbished rooms furnished in classic luxury with marble and tiled bathrooms. Large garage.

A **Jolly de la Gare**, piazza XX Settembre, **T** 051-281611, **F** 051-249764, www.jollyhotels.com *Map 2, E7, p253* A clean and convenient modern chain hotel opposite the train station, bland and comfortable but with the odd period touch. Rooms on the top floors are decidedly more spacious than on the lower floors. The popular restaurant downstairs is open to the public and frequented by locals.

A **Palace**, via Montegrappa 9, **T** 051-237442, **F** 051-220689, www.hotelpalacebologna.com *Map 4, B2, p256* An independent 1930s style hotel in a 17th-century building. Stylish and gracious with mellow wood furnishings and decoration by Raphael in one of the lounges. 113 quiet and sunny rooms with private parking and some, on fifth floor, with great views over rooftops and towers. Ask for the more spacious rooms in the old part of the hotel which also have turn-of-the-century pictures and furniture. Convention room.

A **Sofitel**, viale Pietremellara, **T** 051-248248, **F** 051-249421. *Opposite the station just off piazza delle Medaglie d'oro. Map 2, D7, p253* A modern, well-equipped hotel, popular with businessmen due to conference facilities. The restaurant, Risbo, has a large square turn-of-the-century salon and traditional Bolognese dishes.

B **Astoria**, via Fratelli Rosselli 14, **T** 051-521410, **F** 051-524739, www.astoria.bo.it *Between via Don Minzoni and Giardino G Fava. Map 2, E5, p252* Comfortable modern rooms, 300 m from the station with a garden and inside garage. Bicycles for hire.

B **Due Torri**, via Usberti 4, **T** 051-269826, **F** 051-239944, info@hotelduetorri.it *North of via Ugo Basso near Chiesa di S Colombano. Map 4, B1, 256* 14 recently refurbished rooms 50 m from piazza Maggiore.

B **San Felice**, via Riva Reno 2, **T** 051-557457, **F** 051-558258, www.hotelsanfelice.it *On the corner with via San Felice. Map 2, G2, p252* Quiet and comfortable rooms with modern facilities in an unremarkable building.

C **Atlantic**, via Galliera 46, **T** 051-248488, **F** 051-251538, www.imieiviaggi.com/dim *West of piazza Otto Agosto. Map 2, F7, p253* A simple and economic option situated in one of Bologna's more elegant streets.

C **Cristallo**, via San Giuseppe 5, **T** 051-248574. *West of piazza Otto Agosto, off via dell'Independenza. Map 2, F7, p253* Plain and simple rooms in a convenient location.

C **Metropolitan**, via dell'Orso 6, **T** 051-229393, **F** 051-224602, www.hotelmetropolitan.com *Off via dell'Independenza opposite via Bertiera. Map 2, G7, p253* Refurbished modern and comfortable rooms, most with en-suite facilities.

C **Millennhotel**, via Boldrini 4, **T** 051-6087811, **F** 051-6087888, www.millennhotelbologna.it *One block south of piazza delle Medaglie d'oro, near the station. Map 2, D7, p253* A well-appointed, superior and relatively economical take on functional modern hotels.

C **Nuovo Hotel del Porto**, via del Porto 6, **T** 051-247926, **F** 051-247386, www.nuovohoteldelporto.com *Southeast of piazza dei Martiri. Map 2, E5, p252* A/c rooms with satellite TV in a modern and uninteresting structure but in an interesting revitalized part of town. Mini apartments also available.

D **Marconi**, via Marconi 22, **T** 051-262832. *Opposite the Terminal Alitalia building. Map 2, F7, p253* A rare budget hotel in the old centre, noisy unless you can get a room overlooking the interior.

E **Accogliente Bologna**, via N Sauro 26, **T/F** 051-237498. Three blocks north of via Ugo Bassi. *Map 2, H6, p252* One double room with three beds, one single, separate bathroom, a/c, garage and terrace.

Outskirts of Bologna

B **Best Western**, via A Magenta 10, **T** 051-372676, **F** 051-372032, www.bestwestern.it/city-bo *Map 1, B9, p251* In a nice garden setting between the centre and the fair district, within walking distance of both. Free parking.

C **Garden Hotel**, via Emilia 29, Crespellano, **T** 051-735200. A pleasant and family-run out-of-town hotel in a converted villa. The rooms are spacious, comfortable and tastefully decorated with rustic touches, while the service is courteous and efficient. Breakfast is unusually notable with tasty homemade cakes and jams.

C **Il Guercino**, via L Serra 7, **T** 051-369893, **F** 051-369893, guercino@guercino.it *Map 2, B8, p253* Quiet and budget option close to train station. 30 quiet rooms overlooking an interior courtyard, nice bar and communal areas. Inside parking.

D Il Castello di Galeazza, via Provenone 8585, 40014 Galeazza Pepoli di Crevalcore, www.galeazza.com *north of Bologna*. More of a community retreat than a hotel, this 14th-century castle has 100 rooms and is home to the cultural association, *Reading Retreats in Rural Italy*. It has a library with some 3000 books in English and is also known locally for its classical and jazz concerts and exhibitions. Guests cook, clean and even garden together, thereby reducing the cost of one night's stay to just €40. This is a beautiful escape, only 40 minutes from Bologna.

Agriturismo

Agriturismo is a government-subsidized initiative aimed at supporting the rural economy by promoting lodgings in Italy's countryside.

Cavaione, via Cavaioni 4, Paderno, 6 km south of Bologna, **T** 051-589006, **F** 051-589371, tcavaione@iol.it *Open Mar-Dec*. This 1970s villa offers beautiful views from a rustic setting. It has three large, comfortable doubles, with two shared bathrooms, €25-30 per head per night. Breakfast is extra. You can also rent apartments by the week (€25 per person per day). Guided tours and horseriding are also offered.

Fondo Belfiore, via dei Colli 39, 4 km from Bologna, **T** 051-589400, www.locandabelfiore.com. Open again after a complete refit in 2003. Panoramic views.

Camping

The two nearest campsites are **Piccolo Paradiso**, 15 km away at Sasso Marconi, **T** 051-842680, and **Ca'lescope**, 25 km out of the city in Marzabotto, open to naturists only. Both are open all year round. For other possibilities check www.emiliaromagnaturismo.it.

Camping Hotel – Citta di Bologna, via Romita 12/4, **T** 051-325016, **F** 051-325318, www.hotelcamping.com *Northern end of via Stalingrado*. A relative oasis in a verdant setting near the fiera district. A cross between a hotel and a campsite with more facilities than you could need for camping, including a swimming pool.

Youth hostels

There are two youth hostels 6 km outside the city. *Buses 36 and 37 from the station. Curfew 2330.* **San Sisto**, via Vaidagola 14, **T** 051-519 202, is the older, while **Due Torri**, via Viadagola 5, **T** 051-501810, was purpose-built for passing backpackers.

Around Bologna

Parma

A Hotel Torre, via Ghirardi 8, San Michele Torre, Felino, **T** 0521-831491. A romantic 16th-century castle-like hotel. Small and intimate with 12 rooms in a wonderful setting. Good restaurant.

B Hotel Verdi, viale Pasini 18, **T** 0521-293539. Opposite parco Ducale, this elegant Liberty-syle hotel has refined, marble interiors.

C Croce di Malta, borgo Palmia 8, **T** 0521-235643. Central and predictable, but comfortable. Also has a decent restaurant.

Modena

A Canalgrande, corso Calagrande 6, **T** 059-217160. Located in a 17th-century, neoclassical palazzo with marble column and frescoes, this hotel has all mod cons and comfortable rooms.

C **Liberta**, via Blasia 10, **T** 059-222365. A newly refurbished and efficient hotel plum in the centre.

C **Principe**, corso V Emanuele II, 94, **T** 059-218670.
Well-appointed rooms in an elegant palazzo in the old centre.

Ferrara

A **San Paolo**, via Baluardi 13, **T** 0532-762040. Comfortable and clean accommodation in a nice location by the river.

D **Casa degli Artisti**, via Vittoria 66, **T** 0532-761038. Simple but charming rooms in the medieval quarter.

Imola

C **Molino Rosso**, via Statale Selice 49, **T** 054-640300. A family-run and friendly if unspectacular hotel with a decent restaurant.

Rimini

LL **Rimini** , parco F Fellini 1, **T** 0541-56000. The prestigious seaside address. Luxurious rooms, sports facilities, cool restaurant.

A **Esedra**, viale Caio Duilio, **T** 0541-23421. Journey back in time to turn-of-the-century spa days. Gracious salons, a garden and pool.

D **Biancamano**, via Cappellini 1, **T** 0541-55491. All mod cons for maximum comfort, with ample parking, gardens and a pool.

Eating and drinking

Bologna is to food what Milan is to fashion. The city strains with restaurants in the same way that your belt might after you have spent a few days helplessly gorging yourself on the typically abundant and delicious food. Although famous internationally for its cuisine, Italy is a land full of deeply felt regional identities, where local food specialities are the expression of a region's identity. It is not unusual to hear Italians from different areas claiming theirs to be the home of the best food in Italy. Rich, substantial and varied, *la cucina bolognese* has a better claim than most, something of which the *bolognesi* will lose no opportunity to remind you. But, whatever your view, suffice it to say that food here is taken (and eaten) seriously and copiously; in a city with street names such as vicolo Baciadame (Lady-kisser Lane) and via Fregatette (Tit-rubbing Street) food is enjoyed with gastro-erotic pleasure. And as the city's nickname *la grassa* (the fat) suggests, you are unlikely to go home anything other than totally sated and, certainly, no thinner.

Eating places range from the formal *ristorante,* to the more homely and rustic *trattoria,* to the famous lively pub-like *osteria,* although several have adopted such prefixes in search of *ye olde* authenticity and there are many hybrids that blur these distinctions. The majority of places, instead of cutting-edge design, share variations on the same typical decor of wooden beams and vaulted ceilings and the old values of homemade, handmade dishes prepared with fresh, local, seasonal produce, according to recipes handed down over generations. Don't be surprised if you are not presented with a menu. Chefs will usually take pride in insouciantly reeling off the huge range of dishes on offer and, provided the ingredients are in season, will often be able (and proud) to rustle up anything (Italian) you may ask for, with characteristic *disinvoltura.*

Despite the abundance of restaurants, it is advisable to book ahead. Watch out for days when restaurants are closed and, if visiting in August, be prepared for many restaurants to be closed for holidays. Lunch is usually served between 1200 and 1500 and most places will not open in the evening before 2000, with their kitchens closing at around 2300. In Rimini, Spanish hours are fashionable at the height of summer and restaurants tend to fill up around 2330. Late-night munchies can be satisfied in many *osterie.* It is worth noting that there are fantastic restaurant options outside the Centro Storico and in the surrounding hills. These are accessible by taxi and provide a change from the porticoes and vaults, sometimes with spectacular vistas.

Open to influence and invention, Bologna is better stocked than many Italian cities with ethnic restaurants (Indian, Chinese, Greek and Middle Eastern), which can make a refreshing change from the feasts of regional fare.

Centre: piazza Maggiore and around

Restaurants

€€€ **Pappagallo**, piazza Mercanzia 3, **T** 051-231200. *Closed Sun. Map 5, D9, p256* One of the city's most famous restaurants. In the heart of medieval Bologna set in the walls of an old 14th-century palazzo right underneath the two towers, this historic and elegant restaurant, in a single high-ceilinged, echoing hall, has an accordingly formal and refined atmosphere (although this is rather detracted from by the sycophantic display of self-reverential photographs at eye level). The menu offers a variety of Mediterranean dishes as well as the Bolognese classics and a fine selection of local wines and after-dinner liqeurs.

€€€ **Rodrigo**, via della Zecca 2, **T** 051-235536. *Closed Sun. Map 4, C1, 256* Located in the building that was formerly the National Mint, Rodrigo has been a restaurant for 50 years, serving international and local dishes in a refined environment of wall-to-wall wine bottles (the wine list is accordingly varied and extensive) and chandeliers. Popular for after-show and late-night diners, it is particularly renowned for its white truffles, porcini and agaric mushrooms between September and December.

€€ **Da Gianni – A la Vecia Bulagna**, via Clavature 18, **T** 051-229434. *Closed Mon and also Sun evenings in summer. Map 4, E5, p256* Small and rustic, this is another of Bologna's institutions that has remained unchanged since the 1950s. Fresh hand-made pasta, excellent *bollito misto*, polpettone and *fritto misto*, to be washed down with a fine locally produced San Giovese or Albana. When in season try the chestnut tortelloni.

Trattorie

€ **Tamburini**, via Caprarie 1, T 051-234726, www.tamburini.com *Mon-Fri 1200-1430, also Sat in winter. Map 4, D5, p256* Set in the back of Bologna's most mouth-watering fresh food shops is a simple self-service canteen, where you can sample your own tailor-made selection of the hanging garden of delicacies spread out around the shop and wash them down with a pitcher of draught wine. It is usually packed at lunchtime so if you can bear to wait a little you will be able to eat in peace. Deliveries can be arranged to any address within Italy. Parties can also be organized here.

Cafés

Torinese, piazza re Enzo 1a, T 051-236743. *Map 4, D4, p256* Arguably home of the best hot chocolate in town.

Rosa Rose, piazza Re Enzo. *Map 4, D4, p256* The sister café to the trendy bar-restaurant in via Clavature this is a chic new bar with animal print sofas and designer lamps.

Roxy Bar, via Rizzoli 9, T 051-233746. *Map 4, D5, p256* Immortalized in a song by the famous local-born Italian rocker, Vasco Rossi, this bar is a place of pilgrimage for his fans as the graffiti in the shrine-like toilets testifies. Under the arcades beneath the two towers, this is a small and unremarkable but good place

! The cappuccino is named after the Capuchin monks. They didn't invent it – the coffee is named after their habit of brown cloaks with white hoods.

to start the day. In the evening, in tune with the song's lyrics, it is known for its selection of whisky, port and sherry. Translated as 'A Life on the Edge', *Una Vita Spericolata* by Bologna-born rocker, Vasco Rossi became the angst anthem for Italian youth in the late 1980s. In it the singer tells of his desire to shake free from the claustrophobic conservatism of modern Italy, dare a little and have the life of a film character, specifically 'a life like Steve McQueen'. The chorus then dreams of how he would meet up in the Roxy Bar in Bologna with his friends, all similarly would-be McQueens, and exchange tales of their exploits.

Northeast: the university quarter

Restaurants

€€€ **Franco Rossi**, via Goito 3, **T** 051-238818. *Closed Sun except during trade fairs*. *Map 4, A4, p256* More of an exclusive drawing room this small and welcoming restaurant is a delight, both for its quiet and intimate atmosphere and for its slightly lighter and more modern take on heavy Bolognese traditions. Franco will serve and advise you while his brother Lino works magic behind the scenes.

€€ **Benso**, vicolo San Giobbe 3, **T** 051-223904. *Closed Sun*. *Map 4, C5, p256* Tucked down an intriguing little passage on the edge of the old Jewish ghetto this is a fun restaurant. A series of interlinked sexily-lit little rooms are always full and popular with footballers and fans of Bologna FC (as you can tell by the decor and strange murals) especially the day after a match. It is a famous

! The original recipe for spaghetti bolognese is a far cry from the bastardized international version. It should contain beef, bacon, carrots, celery, onions, tomato sauce, dry white wine, and whole milk. The correct local name is *tagliatelle al ragu*.

▶ Regional specialities

Broadly speaking the region's cuisine can be divided in two: Emilia, the western part is known for its cured meats and cheeses, while Romagna in the east has a variety of elaborate fish dishes.

By way of an *antipasto* (starter) there are almost as many kinds of *salami* and *prosciutto* as there are towns. The world-famous *prosciutto* of Parma should not obscure other variants on the cold meat theme such as *culatello* also from Parma, *mortadella* from Bologna, *zampone* (stuffed pig's trotter) from Modena and *pancetta* and *coppa* (both types of ham) from Piacenza.

On the side, to help you assuage your hunger before the main dishes arrive, you will probably be offered *cresentine*, delicious, poppadum-like discs, usually topped with mozzarella and mortadella.

For the *primo piatto*, Bologna is the home of stuffed pastas, such as *tortellini, cappellacci,* and *anolini,* as well as the old favourite, *lasagne*.

The famous cheese of Parma, *parmigiano,* is an essential ingredient; not only to sprinkle on top of your pasta but also, when added to milk, to make the many sauces and baked pasta dishes *alla parmigiana,* which define the region's cooking. Parmesan is not the region's only cheese, however, and visitors should try the equally pungent *grana padano* and also the beautifully soft cow's milk *squacquerone*.

On your side salad, drizzle a little *aceto balsamico* (balsamic vinegar) from Modena, and wash it all down with a glass of Lambrusco, Albana or Sangiovese.

Hearty eaters might be tempted to find room for a delectable dessert, from the almondy and crunchy *torta sbrisolona,* or spiced *spongata* (sponge cake) to the *torta di riso* (rice cake), or the perversely named *zuppa inglese* (English soup), which we simply call trifle.

restaurant founded in 1903 and now owned by Beppe and Piero who stick to Bolognese traditional cuisine for the main courses while their southern roots come through in unmissable desserts like *gelato ripieno all frutta* and *cassata siciliana*. There is an interior garden for eating outside in summer.

€€ **Bentivoglio**, via Mascarella, 4/B, **T** 051-265416, www.affari. com/bentivoglio *2000-0200. Closed Mon.* *Map 4, C5, p256* Set in a basement evocative of the cellars of the Bentivoglio palace this is the best place to hear live jazz. The Ronnie Scott's of Bologna and something of an institution in the city, the slightly disappointing food (relatively speaking, of course – this is Bologna) is compensated for by the quality of the music, the appropriately cool ambience and an extensive wine list of over 400 labels. Advisable to book, especially at weekends and if you want to eat late. See website for information on visiting artists and full programme. Short cookery courses sometimes offered.

€€ **Doge**, via Caldarese 5, **T** 051-227980. *Closed Mon.* *Map 4, D7, p256* Slightly kitsch but air-conditioned setting with tasty pizzas and Mediterranean food and fresh fish every day.

€€ **Donatello**, via Righi 8, **T** 051-235438. *Closed Sat.* *Map 2, G8, p253* An elegant restaurant with high frescoed ceilings and traditional furnishings that has been open since 1903. The menu offers a vast choice of dishes with the local specialities of boiled meat being particular tasty among the *secondi*. Try the slices of beef in balsamic vinegar. The walls tell of 100 years of popularity among famous artists and musicians, from Puccini to Bocelli. The restaurant is still often frequented by sports and showbiz personalities.

! Bolognese legend says that *tortellini* are the creation of a Roman inn-keeper who, overawed by the beauty of Venus' navel, was inspired to create a pasta in its image.

★ **Cheap eats**

Best
- La Mariposa, p140
- Trattoria Serghei, p140
- Osteria dell'Orsa, p141
- Grassilli, p145
- Trattoria al 15, p146

€€ **Pino**, via Goito 2, **T** 051-227291. *Closed Mon. Map 4, A4, p256* Wood oven-cooked pizzas and fresh Bolognese cuisine with handmade pasta. Outside veranda during the summer.

€ **Da Matusel**, via Bertoloni 2, **T** 051-231718. *Closed Sat lunchtime and Sun. Map 2, G10, 253* Meaning 'Mad Bird', this was once a popular and noisy bar near the university. It is now a modern restaurant, serving all types of generic Mediterranean food.

€ **Marsalino**, via Marsala, 13/d, **T** 051-238 675. *Closed Mon, 1200-0200. Map 4, B7, p256* Cosy restaurant-cum-café with great specials and good wine. Very small so get there early, especially for the cabaret/live music nights on Thursdays, which have become very popular.

Trattorie

€€ **Annamaria**, via delle Belle Arti 17, **T** 051-266894. *Closed Mon. Map 4, A8, p256* Set just behind the Teatro Comunale in the lively university district, this famous and hospitable restaurant is often frequented by actors and 'VIP' from Italian showbiz, a fact to which the photographs emblazoned all over the walls play testament. The menu is rooted in Bolognese tradition with fresh handmade pastas and sauces centre stage. The *sfogline* can be seen kneading their stuff by day. The speciality is *tortellini alla gorgonzola*. Alernatively try the roast rabbit followed by Bolognese trifle or the crème brûlée.

€ **Il Portico**, via A Righi 11, **T** 051-221185. *Map 2, G8, p253*
A good-value and functional restaurant with a warm decor, nice turn-of-the-century furniture set within a classic arcade. The pizzas are particularly good and the restaurant also offers a more substantial and typical menu.

€ **La Mariposa**, via Bertiera 12, **T** 051-225656. *Closed Sat eve and Sun. Map 2, G8, p253* A genuine and humble trattoria still with its rather kitsch post-war decor. Very welcoming, delicious and superb value. Another taste of the real Bologna.

€ **Le Maschere**, via Zappoli, 5, **T** 051-261 035. *Closed Sun. Map 2, G8, p253* Ingenious and spicy fish recipes combining Romagna with Egypt. Popular and small so book ahead. Specialities lobster, seafood spaghetti or risotto, *coquilles San Jacques*, and squid kebabs.

€ **Serghei**, via Piella 12, **T** 051-233533. *Closed Sat eve and Sun. Map 2, H8, p253* Originally started as a salon for card players who wanted a bit of a snack this small and honest trattoria has lost nothing of its origins. It serves wholesome, simple and abundant Bolognese dishes, perfect for famished students. Now run by the second generation family, Serghei was the nickname a group of regular visiting Russian dancers gave their father in the 60s.

€ **Toni**, via Augusto Righi 1, **T** 051-232852. *Closed Mon and Tue. Map 2, G7, p253* Easy-going pub-bar nicely stuck in the past and serving robust Bolognese classics at decent prices.

Osterie

€ **Dell'Orsa**, via Mentana 1, **T** 051-231576. *Daily until 0100.   Map 4, A6, p256* Popular student lunch hangout serving simple menu of regional dishes all day until 0100. Great crostini and a broad range of beers. Good lively stop for lunch if you want a taste of young Bologna.

€ **Du Madon**, via San Vitale 73, **T** 051-226221. *Closed Sun.   Map 3, A11, p255* Unprepossessing from the outside this is a typical osteria with vaulted brick ceilings and dark wood furnishings offering typically robust and high-quality local dishes.

Greek

€€ **Taverna Partenone**, piazza San Martino 4, **T** 051-230185. *Closed Mon.   Map 4, A6, p256* An informal piece of Greece in a peaceful piazza, serving Bolognese and superior Greek cuisine. Good octopus and fish salads.

€€ **To'steki**, largo Respighi 4, **T** 051-268012. *Closed Sun.   Map 4, A6, p256 Next to Teatro Comunale.* Good for whole meals or snacks – particularly at lunch – this restaurant offers more unusual Greek dishes than the typical fare and a broad range of potent wines.

Indian

€ **Delhi Palace**, vicolo de' Facchini 4, **T** 051-221920, www.delhipalace.it *Map 4, A7, p256* Replacing the Buddah Thai restaurant, the Delhi Palace offers a full range of genuine Indian cuisine in pleasant surroundings and with affable service.

€€ **Moghul**, via dell'Inferno 16, **T** 051-232911. *Closed Sun. Map 4, B6, p256* A welcoming and atmospheric place, worth a visit for a change of palate.

Middle Eastern

€ **Al Salaam**, via Centotrecento 24, T 051-244173. *Closed Sun. Map 2, G10, p253* A taste of the Middle East under the arcades with falafel, fatayer and mint tea. Jamil, a doctor who originally came to Bologna to get a pharmacy PhD, displays typical Middle Eastern courtesy and offers tailor-made preparations, ringing a bell to say when your dish is ready, the number of rings being the number of your table.

Latin

€€ **Cubano Cohiba**, via Borgo S Pietro 54/a-b, **T** 051-6390527. *Map 2, F9, p253* Cuban cuisine with shows and live music in a lively setting.

€€ **Piedra del Sol**, via Goito 20, **T** 051-236151/051-227229. *Closed Tue. Map 4, A5, p256* An air of the tropics in downtown Bologna. A lively place offering superior Mexican cuisine, shows and music. Packed at weekends so be prepared to queue and try one their excellent margaritas while you wait.

Cafés

Bravo, via Mascarella 1, **T** 051-266112. *Daily 1230-1530, 1900-0200. Map 4, A8, p256* A must for Sunday brunch, served 1200-1600, where for a reasonable flat price you can eat as much as want from a delicious smorgasbord of cold Bolognese dishes, soups and cakes in hip contemporary surroundings with Bologna's

Coffee houses

•Caffe la Torinese, p135
•Caffe del Teatro, p143
•Caffe Terzi, p144
•Caffe de' Commercianti, p148
•Caffe Morandi, p148.

affluent youth. In a bizarre statement of retro irony in this coffee-proud country Nescafé is the height of fashion here, served up by waitresses looking like Malboro girls. An Italian take on the greasy spoon and a great place to eat off a hangover.

Del Museo, via Zamboni 58, **T** 051-246620. *Early closing Sat. Closed Aug. Happy 'hour' Thu, 1830-2230. Map 2, H11, p253* Welcoming and retro, dark wood, sofas, alcoves and mirrors, great for tête-à-tête and romantic drinks served by Felix the funny barman. Popular with work-shy students and professors.

Del Teatro, via Zamboni 26, **T** 051-222623. *Map 4, B8, p256* Opposite Teatro Comunale and supposedly the place where the *festa della laurea* (graduation party) was invented. Enjoy the pleasant and decadent atmosphere.

Del Rosso, via A Righi 30, **T** 051-236730. *Closed Mon. Map 2, G8, p253* Open since 1850 this place has a sombre and slightly empty atmosphere but the old building retains many of its original features. Local specialities and very good *crescentine* and *tigelle*.

Golem caffe d'Arte, piazza San martino 3/b, **T** 051-262620. *Closed Sun eve. Map 4, A6, p256* In the heart of the old Jewish quarter this is a classy all-in-one joint, popular with artists and intellectuals. There are art exhibits on the walls as well as books, newspapers and boardgames for customers. The bar also hosts live music, films, and small theatre productions, and serves fine cocktails and a decent menu. Effete, expensive but ultimately cool.

Terzi, via Oberdan, 10, **T** 051-236470. *Map 4, C5, p256* Recently opened, this sophisticated café aims to recreate the experience of the coffee salons of Paris and Venice, but offers an untypical selection of coffees and teas. The cappuccinos come served with mouthwatering fresh gratings of dark chocolate. There is also a recherché selection of fine wines and, slightly more pretentiously, different waters, all of which can be consumed either at the bar or in the small but stylish salon at the back. A great place for a luxurious breakfast if you're staying at the Hotel Corona d'Oro.

Whoopie, via Oberdan 24, **T** 051-271618. *Map 4, A5, p256* Popular café in this pedestrian street with outside tables. For a drink, snack or aperitif.

Southeast: Santo Stefano and around

Restaurants

€€€ **Antica Osteria Romagnola**, via Rialto 13, **T** 051-263699. *Closed all day Mon and Tue at midday. Map 3, D9, p255* Comfortingly anonymous from the outside Antonio's restaurant is rustic, welcoming and always noisy, with dark wood panels, musical instruments and mirrors on the walls, and a characteristic inner courtyard. Superb local and regional cuisine tailor-made to your taste. Particularly tasty mortadella *a cubetti* and lasagne. Occasionally the meal is accompanied by a pianist.

€€€ **Drogheria della Rosa**, via Cartoleria 10, **T** 051-266 864/ 051-222 529. *Closed Sun. Map 3, D9, p255* This cosy restaurant run by the ebullient Emanuele Addone used to be a food store (hence its name) and still retains the original furnishings, doors and window frames. Superior dishes from all over Emilia-Romagna are served in an intimate atmosphere with an exceptional choice of wines. The mozzarella alone is beautifully juicy and sweet.

€€€ **L'Anatra e l'Arancia**, via Rolandino 1, **T** 051-225505. *Closed Sun. Map 3, C7, p254* Literally 'the duck and the orange' this atmospheric and young-spirited restaurant is more Romagna than Emilia, mostly based on seafood with the odd innovative fusion such as pate de foie gras with shellfish. All dishes come served with *piadina*, the traditional Romagna bread.

€€ **Cesarina**, via Santo Stefano 19, **T** 051-232037. *Closed all Mon and Tue lunch. Map 4, F7, p256* Set in the arcades overlooking arguably the most tranquil and picturesque square in Bologna, Cesarina offers specialities from all over Emilia-Romagna and particularly good fish dishes such as *Maltagliati* with moscardini fish, and has an impressive selection of international wines and spirits to match. The speciality of the house is cannellone stuffed with thin tagliatelle, porcini mushrooms and parmesan.

€€ **Da Fabio**, via del Cestello 2, **T** 051-220481. *Eves only. Closed Sun. Map 3, E9, p255* Wonderful and plentiful regional dishes in this cosy, intimate and unpreposessing little restaurant with personal service.

€€ **Maria Café**, via Cartoleria 15, **T** 051-272900. *Map 3, D9, p255* Opposite the Teatro Duse and set in a quiet, romantic porticoed street, this is a favourite with thespians. It's got a new name but traditional, regional dishes are still the speciality.

€ **Grassilli**, via del Luzzo 3, **T** 051-222961. *Closed Wed. Map 4, D6, p256* Tucked away in an obscure part of the city this is a rare 'fusion food' restaurant in Bologna where the transalpine ideas of French chef Jacques Durussel meet Emilian traditions to surprising effect, and with a respect rare in these parts for the calorific concerns of the day. Traditionally attracts musicians and composers. With excellent service, this is one for special occasions. Book ahead.

Trattorie and others

€€ **Al 15 (Quindici)**, via Mirasole 15, **T** 051-331806. *Closed Sun.* *Map 3, E6, p254*   Currently popular with a young and lively clientele. Abundant portions of Bolognese cuisine. Try the *crescentini* and the *tortelloni ai carciofi* (artichokes). Simple decor, newspapers on ceilings and refreshingly informal and insouciant service. Try and eat in the back room. Best to book.

€€ **Da Ercole**, piazza Minghetti 2, **T** 051-228848. *Closed Mon.* *Map 4, F5, p256*   Situated on a leafy piazza here you will find typical Bolognese cuisine, good fish dishes and large salads. Perfect for a lunch stop and popular with older locals with seating outside in the summer. Ercole (Hercule if you're Belgian) also runs a few bed and breakfast rooms upstairs (www.bedandbreakfastinbologna.it)

€€ **Leonida**, vicolo Alemagna 2, **T** 051-239742. *Closed Sun.* *Map 4, E6, p256*   Warm and mellow arts and crafts wooden interior. Sumptuous meat dishes with vegetable accompaniments and sauces according to the season. Particularly good asparagus lasagne, peas with tagliatelle and other delicious pasta dishes with artichokes and aubergines when in season.

€€ **Trebbi**, via Solferino 40, **T** 051-583713. *Closed Sat lunch.* *Map 3, D6, p254*   One of Bologna's historic trattorias, open for over 50 years and serving simple local fare that seems to go down well with late-night stragglers and their drink.

€ **Bottega Albertini**, via dei Coltelli, 9/2, **T** 051-228 532. *Closed Sun*. *Map 3, E10, p255* Formerly the Sale e Pepe restaurant, this establishment serves creative cuisine, specializing in non-traditional dishes such as cream puff with hot chocolate in a romantic candle-lit setting. The fixed price of €15 per head for a meal including wine makes this one of the best deals in town.

Osterie

€€€ **Dei Poeti**, via dei Poeti 1, **T** 051-236166. *Closed Mon*. *Map 3, C8, p255* Another of Bologna's oldest osterias located in the 14th-century Palazzo Senatorio. It owes its modern name to the custom of the Bolognese poets Carducci and Pascoli and could perhaps be accused of resting on their laurels. There are two rooms: one smaller with a fireplace and the larger where three times a week there is live music. Besides the excellent choice of Italian wines you can feast on typically wholesome Bolognese fare.

€€ **Degli Angeli**, via Farini 31, **T** 051-268032. *Closed Sat lunch and all Sun*. *Map 3, C9, p255* In this little 'tavern of the angels' you can eat like the gods even if the pleasure of the food seems sinful – in particular the lamb cutlets . All will be forgiven.

€€ **Le Mura**, via Falcone, 13, **T** 051-331772. *Closed Mon*. *Map 3, E6, p254* Although it's 15 minutes walk from the centre, its location just inside the perimeter mean this simple, lively and informal restaurant is largely ignored by tourists. Typical Bolognese fare is served in generous portions and without ceremony. Great for entertaining large groups. Book in advance.

€€ **L'Infedele**, via Gerusalemme 5, **T** 051-239456. *Closed Mon*. *Map 4, E7, p256* Small bohemian joint with classic snacks and some *primi piatti* for those with more of a twist.

Eating and drinking

Vegetarian

€ **Clorofilla**, strada Maggiore 64, **T** 051-235343. *Closed Sun. Map 3, C11, p255* One of Bologna's few lifestyle-eating propositions with a minimalist-naturalist decor this restaurant offers healthy dishes mixing ingredients from all round the world complete with explanations of their healthy properties. Particularly big on salads which might provide light relief for non-vegetarians. There is a wide selections of teas and tisanes, and even the beer and wine are organic.

Cafés and gelaterie

Bricco d'Oro, via Farini 6, **T** 051-236231. *Map 3, C7, p255* Very good hot chocolate topped with mountainous cream. Also a broad selection of bites at aperitif time.

Dei Commercianti, strada Maggiore 23/c, **T** 051-266539. *Mon-Sat until 2200 Map 4, D7, p256* This place used to serve extra special and varied coffees – writer Umberto Eco and ex-prime minister Prodi even used to drink here – but now it's just another trendy, minimalist café, popular with up-and-coming arty types and British Council teachers. Still a great spot for *frizzantini* and tiny crustless sandwiches, however, and also popular at aperitif time.

Morandi, piazzetta Morandi 1, **T** 051-342734. *Map 3, D12, p255* An anonymous bar that serves perhaps the best cappuccino in town: thick and creamy and full of flavour due to a slightly more patient preparation than elsewhere.

Zanarini, piazza Galvani 1, **T** 051-261891. *Map 3, C7, p255* Still closed for long-term refurbishment but previously famous for its long drinks, pastries, cakes, great coffee and for its elegant salon, with period furnishings and sofas. Worth a visit if it ever reopens.

Gelaterias

Sorbetteria Castiglione, via Castiglioni 44, **T** 051-233257.
1730-2345. *Closed Tue. Map 3, E9, p255* Locals will cross the
entire town for the ice-creams here, which are just that bit
creamier, subtler and naughtier than elsewhere. Highly
recommended late at night.

Southwest: around via del Pratello

Restaurants

€€€ **Trattoria Battibecco**, via Battibecco 4, **T** 051-2232298.
Closed lunchtime Sat and all day Sun. Map 4, D2, p256
Only a trattoria by name in order to evoke a sense of tradition,
make no mistake, this is one of Bologna's most expensive and
luxurious restaurants, as far away from a trattoria as can be.
The decor is sophisticated with a wooden ceiling, tiled floor
and trompe l'oeil walls with backlit recesses. There's no denying
the sumptuousness of its predominantly fish-based dishes, which
are mix of traditional and experimental, all served in a refined
atmosphere tucked away in a quiet narrow street in the heart
of the historic centre.

€€€ **Biagi alla Grada**, via della Grada 6, **T** 051-553025.
Closed Tue. Map 2, H2, p252 Open since 1937 and still in the
hands of the founding Biagi family this traditional elegant
restaurant offers typical Bolognese cuisine cooked to perfection.
By common consent the tortellini, handmade by the corpulent
Signor Biagi whose size is testament to fine living, are the best
in town.

€€ **Amedeo**, via Saragozza 88, **T** 051-585060, *Closed Sun. Map 3, D3, p254* This is a lovely restaurant with tables underneath the porticoes popular with students celebrating graduation. Amedeo is originally from Basilicata in the south of Italy but the cuisine here is all Bolongese with one or two inventions in the *secondi*.

€€ **Cesari**, via Carbonesi 8, **T** 051-237710. *Closed Sun, also Sat in summer. Map 3, C6, p254* A warm welcome awaits here in a resplendent inner room complete with a cast-iron chandelier and antique engravings. The menu is a reliable, standard choice of typical local and regional food.

Trattorie

€€ **Della Santa**, via Urbana 7, **T** 051-330415. *Closed Sun. Map 3, C5, p254* Another typical Bolognese trattoria but a highlight in its vast gastronomic landscape serving fresh homemade tortelloni and tagliatelle in a typical arcaded building with a wood-beamed ceiling. Nice informal service. Book ahead.

€€ **Meloncello**, via Saragozza 240, **T** 051-6143947. *Closed Mon eve and Tue. Map 3, C2, p254* Superbly positioned in the corner of the city leading out through Porta Saragozza, this old trattoria has, for years, provided sustenance for those who are about to make the pilgrimage up the porticoes to San Luca or restored them coming down. Intimate and a little bit musty, it really feels like the extension of an Italian family home with a dedicated clientele of regulars. The rabbit with polenta is delicious and stuffed zucchini a speciality. Essential to book ahead during the festival of San Luca in May. Ask for a table in the tiny backroom which is also non-smoking.

Osterie

€€ **Due Porte**, via del Pratello 62, **T** 051-523565. *Closed Tue.*
Map 3, A2, p254 A homely tavern serving Bolognese and southern
pasta dishes with a broad selection of wines from all over Italy.

€€ **La Traviata**, via Urbana, 5/C, **T** 051-331298. *Mon-Fri for lunch.*
Mon-Sat for dinner. Map 3, C4, p254 Not surprisingly a musical
theme reigns in this informal bar, with old instruments hung on
the walls. Its low lights, dark wood and informal atmosphere as
well as simple but tasty dishes make it popular with young locals.

€€ **Montesino**, via del Pratello 74, **T** 051-523426. *Closed Mon.*
Map 3, A2, p254 Congenial hangout for good food and wine, with
a leaning towards the Sardinian roots of the owner. A quiet place
as the owner will not accept groups. The poems written on the
table cloths are reputedly published in a tri-annual collection.

€€ **Ribalta**, viaM d'Azeglio 41, **T** 051-331101. *Map 3, D6, p254*
A charming spot with walls covered in posters of old Bologna.

€ **Bass' Otto Cafeteria**, via Ugo Bassi 8, **T** 051-232511. *Closed
weekends. Map 4, C1, p256* A modern and noisy bistro ideal for a
quick and inexpensive meal.

€ **Brancaleone**, via Santa Caterina 51, **T** 051-585111. *Closed Sun
and Mon. Map 3, C3, p254* A candlelit and intimate pub-bar with a
limited but tasty range of dishes from the Abruzzi region.

€ **Cantinone**, via del Pratello, 56/A, **T** 051-553223. *Closed Wed.*
Map 3, A3, p254 On a road famous for its high concentration of
bars, this is one that since the 70s heyday has been popular among
students and cheaper as a result. A quirky place with a broad

selection of soups and wines and also just about any product you can make from milk. Not so hot on the beer.

€ **Fantoni**, via del Pratello 11 **T** 051-236358. *Closed Sun and also Mon eve.* *Map 3, A4, p254* An old-style trattoria serving very good value Bolognese food on a picturesque ancient street with views onto chiesa San Francesco and the piazza.

€ **Senzanome**, 42 via Senzannome /A, **T** 051-331147. *Closed Mon.* *Map 3, C4, p254* Delicious tripe and dishes with beans. Pleasant, simple old-world ambience, open until late.

Indian

€€ **Taj Mahal**, via San Felice 92, **T** 051-524894. *Closed Tue.* *Map 2, G2, p252* The most informal and economical of Bologna's Indian options. It doesn't try to recreate a full-on Indian atmosphere but does offer typically friendly Indian service.

Cafés and gelaterie

Majani, via De' Carbonesi 5, **T** 051-234302. *Map 3, C6, p254* A Bolognese institution and the sweet equivalent of Tamburini: an elegant and mouth-watering art nouveau shrine to the city's famous chocolate-maker Signora Majani, as it was when the shop was founded in 1834. For the proverbial child in a sweet-shop.

Pielle, via San Felice 13, **T** 051-224461. *Map 2, H4, p252* All kinds of manna: liqueurs, oils, honeys and freshly ground coffee.

Ugo, via San Felice 24, **T** 051-263849. *Map 2, H4, p252* According to many locals the best gelato in town and certainly rightfully famous for high-quality creamy licks.

Northwest: around via Galliera

Restaurants

€€€ **Carracci**, via Manzoni 2, **T** 051-222049. *Mon-Sun*.
Map 4, B3, p256 This famous restaurant is located within the
premises of the Grand Hotel Baglioni, the luxury address for visitors
to Bologna. The restaurant itself is set in a magnificent hall with
frescoes by artists from the Carracci school whose name it bears.
The atmosphere is refined and the menu covers local specialities as
well as many international dishes. Sadly, there have been recent
reports of snooty service and a suggestion that the kitchen is
resting on its laurels.

€€€ **Diana**, via dell dell'Indipendenza 24, **T** 051-231302. *Closed
Mon. Map 2, H7, p253* Part of the establishment since the 1920s
this elegant and sophisticated restaurant, complete with crystal
chandeliers is one for gourmets wanting to appreciate the finer
nuances in the local cuisine. The *Dindo Diana* (turkey) and the
chicken galantine are the restaurant's signature main courses
while the apple meringue cake is an unmissable pudding.

€€€ **Luciano**, via N Sauro 19, **T** 051-231249. *Closed Wed.*
Map 2, H6, p252 Art Nouveau style restaurant, supposedly a
combination of osteria and ristorante. A lovely and original place,
perfect for an intimate tête-à-tête. The mellow wood interior has
dimmed lighting and little alcoves for privacy. Great for a quiet
lunch stop with good soups, chicken, homely pasta dishes and
tempting dolci. Relatively expensive.

€€ **Caminetto d'Oro**, via dei Falegnami 4, **T** 051-263494,
www.caminettodoro.it *Closed Tue eve and Wed. Map 2, G7, p253*
A traditional family-run restaurant next to the Arena del Sole

popular with artists and actors. Meat is cooked on an open fire in winter. The menu combines the best of tradition with innovation using local and seasonal produce for maximum taste. The rigatoni with shallots and *sogliano fossa* cheese are memorable.

€€ **Il Pirata del Porto,** via del Porto 42, **T** 051-552750. *Closed Mon. Map 2, E5, p252* A new and popular seafood option in the upcoming former port and industrial sector of the city. Large and airy and always busy at weekends and at lunch time.

€€ **Montegrappa "da Nello"**, via Montegrappa 2, **T** 051-236331. *Closed Mon. Map 4, B3, p256* Despite its small entrance this is a large and cavernous restaurant which is nearly always oversubscribed. It serves very specific local dishes, according to their town of origin. A good place to witness the pride and different tastes of meats cured only kilometres away from each other.

€€ **Paranza**, piazza VII Novembre 2, **T** 051-522002. *Closed Mon. Map 2, E3, p252* Good value fish dishes and seafood inspired by southern Italian recipes. Not particularly exciting from outside but welcoming inside with colourful tiles.

Osterie

€€ **Da Pietro**, via Falegnami 18, **T** 051-230644. *Closed Sun except during festivals. Map 2, G7, p253* Intimately spaced tables on two floors provide for a cosy atmosphere and there are tables outside under the arcades with heaters during spring and autumn. The menu is a mixture of Umbrian and Bolognese cuisine with a small list of local wines and great puddings.

€€ **Piazza Grande**, via Manzoni 6, **T** 051-265786. *Closed Tue. Map 4, B3, p256* Open until late this osteria is popular with good-timers and gourmets. Its ancient wood-beamed ceiling makes it almost a piece of urban archaeology, adding authenticity to the delicious Emilian dishes on the menu.

€ **C'entro**, via dell'Indipendenza 45, **T** 051-234216. *Closed Sun. Map 2, G7, p253*   Fast food without losing the tradition and taste. As a modern self-service canteen concept this place is very different from the majority of the city's restaurants. Popular during the week for a quick working lunch, the mass catering still retains its base in local traditions and offers a huge choice of very tasty dishes.

Chinese

€ **Fortuna**, via Morgagni 8, **T** 051-266914. *Closed Wed. Map 2, H5, p252*   A well-established and respected restaurant offering typical Chiense and Vietnamese dishes in a decor to match.

Indian

€€ **India**, via N Sauro14, **T** 051-271095. *Closed Mon. Map 4, B1, p256*   Not your average curry house, this Italian take on the Indian experience does not suffer from student stereotyping. The decor is sophisticated, detailed and well-conceived while the chefs are two Indians offering both tandoori and mughlai dishes. From Tuesday to Friday there is an excellent and highly recommended buffet lunch allowing you to taste as much as you want from a whole range of dishes for a very acceptable fixed price of €12.

Cafés

Altero, via dell'Indipendenza 33, **T** 051-234758. *Map 2, G7, p253*   One of a chain of snack bars reliable for good pizza *al taglio* (by the slice). There is also a branch at via Ugo Bassi 10, **T** 051-226612.

Calderoni, via dell'Indipendenza 70, **T** 051-248208. *Map 2, E8 p253* A popular bar on this main street. Downstairs a range of pastas, salads and cakes are on display. In the late afternoons the upstairs turns into a piano bar serving decent cocktails and delicious ice-creams.

Duchamp Caffe d'Arte, via N Sauro 12. *Map 4, B1, p256* Very chic Parisian Art-Déco style bistro with a dark wooden interior serving select wines and beers, and a limited range of chic snacks. Expensive but cool.

Impero, via dell'Indipendenza 39, **T** 051-232337. *Map 2, G7, p253* An old pasticceria now part of a chain but still with original furnishings serving delicious croissants and various pastries at all times.

Piccolo, via Riva Reno 114, **T** 051-236389. *Mon-Fri 1000-2000 Map 2, G6, p252* Supposedly Bologna's first 'green' bar this place caters for lovers of all beverages natural and organic: malt cacao, goats milk cappuccino, plum cake with honey and many savoury delights, organic beers, teas and tisanes.

Outskirts of Bologna

Restaurants

€€€ **Acqua Pazza**, via Murri, 168, **T** 051-443422. *Closed Sat lunch and Mon. Southeast of centre beyond piazza Santo Stefano.* Literally translated as 'mad water' this is an interesting and sophisticated small restaurant with more attention to modernism and originality in decor than many of the city's restaurants. There are water themes in the murals and the menu is one for disciples of fish and seafood in sumptuous and surprising sauces and preparations.

€€€ **Del Cacciatore**, via Caduti di Casteldebole 25, **T** 051-564203. *Closed Sun eve and Mon. West of centre along via Emilia Ponente then south before tangenziale*. A large, convivial and country-style restaurant, a favourite with hunters who have inspired its name. A long corridor leads to a vast, beamed hall with spacious and well-spaced tables, while there are siderooms for more privacy and non-smokers. The superb and copious menu is predominantly game, with delicious fresh mushrooms when they are in season, all served with local wines (from a choice of over 300) and, if you need a little help digesting, a broad range of local, label-less grappas.

€€€ **La Bottega di Franco**, via Agucchi 112, **T** 051-311243, **F** 051-388746. *Closed Mon am and Sun. West along via Emilia Ponente then north before river and over railway*. Built at the end of the 17th century, this former country house of a Bolognese Contessa provides an elegant, secluded and bohemian setting for a romantic feast 10 minutes away by taxi from the Centro Storico. Inside the decor is bohemian and undeliberately assembled, almost Parisian with a nod to the cinema. It is no surprise that Franco organizes Murder Mystery evenings on Mondays à la Maigret. Forty people sit on one table with actors sitting among you, the plot thickening with your arteries as the evening unfolds. Otherwise the restaurant has a nice homemade feel with dishes being brought in their casseroles and then taken away as if at home. There are tables outside and Franco plans to develop the cellar downstairs. A secret it pains me to disclose. Book in advance.

€€€ **Panoramica**, via San Mamolo 31, **T** 051-580337. *Closed Sun. South through Porta San Mamolo*. Despite its slightly kitsch faux-liberty 80s decor, this is an agreeable restaurant, especially if you can sit outside on the ground floor veranda or upstairs on the terrace which is conducive to intimate conversation over a nice bottle. Big on delicious salads with mushrooms and artichokes.

€€ Ai Butteri, via Murri 20, **T** 051-347718. *Closed Sun. Southeast beyond Porta San Stefano*. The stereotypical Italian restaurant complete with red-checked table cloths. The cuisine is Tuscan and the gentle giant Augusto will make you feel very at home, and very full. Wash it down with a carafe of *vinsanto* and *cantucci*. It is popular and small so booking ahead is obligatory.

€€ Boni, via don Sturzo 22, **T** 051-6154337. *Closed Sun eve, Mon and half of Jan. Southwest along via Saragozza then fork right along via Porettana towards Casalecchio*. Old-fashioned, family-run trattoria that has been running for over 40 years, lovingly cared for by Antonio and Agnese. Simple and friendly atmosphere and wholesome home cooking.

€€ Dei Picari, via Emilia Ponente 459, **T** 051-6190367. *Closed Sat midday and Sun. West of centre beyond piazza San Felice*. A little-known gem tucked away beneath the via Emilia at the end of the Ponte Marco. Formerly a stables and coach house, the decor is typically tavern-like with assorted objects and rustic wood furnishings. The four different fixed price menus are exceptionally good value and are inclusive of wine. They offer a range of surprising takes on regional themes that attract gourmets from afar – from the sophisticated *tortelloni alle melanzane con pomodoro e mentuccia* to the basic traditional subsistence dish of the Apennine hill folk, pasta in mashed potato and garlic.

€€ Dello Sterlino, via Murri 71, **T** 051-342751. *Closed Tue. Southeast beyond piazza Santo Stefano*. Named after the starlings that used to populate this area before the city's expansion, this is a restaurant, pizzeria and hotel in one. Opened as a restaurant 80 years ago the 17th-century building was once the coach house and stopover point for travellers on their way to Florence and is alleged to have restored Goethe on his travels. Nowadays fine regional food is served to lesser mortals in a rustic setting of three arched rooms.

€€ **Del Pontelungo,** via Emilia Ponente 307, **T** 051-382996. *Closed Sat and Sun. Due west beyond piazza San Felice*. A historic venue as the black and white photos on the walls bear witness to. A jumbled decor of old mirrors with advertisements, modern art and old furniture. You only pay for what you drink, but that will probably be quite a lot as both the wine and the food are delicious.

€ **Da Vito**, via Musolesi 9, San Luca, **T** 051-349809. *Closed Wed. Opposite the basilica of San Luca*. At the top of the long portico this is one of the best pizzerias in town, also renowned for its choice of delicious homemade pastries and cakes, all great value and a reward for anyone who has walked up (or an inspiration to walk down for those who have not). In summer tables are also put out in the inner garden but year round the place offers spectacular views over the whole city.

€ **Paradisino**, via C Vighi 33, **T** 051-566401. *Closed Sun, also Tue except in summer. Closed Jan. West, in Reno, south off viale Palmiro Togliatti*. A wonderful old country house in a beautiful setting surrounded by green, 'the little paradise' offers excellent value open-air lunches (evening meals are usually inside) specializing in local and long-lost traditional recipes that, like most Bolognese cuisine, are not for the faint-hearted or conservationist. Try the *birichini* (little freshwater fish) or the frogs, either fried or stewed, whichever you prefer, fresh from the Reno that flows nearby.

€ **De Monte Donato,** via Siepelunga 118, **T** 051-472901. *Closed Mon. In hills beyond Giardini Margherita out of piazza Castiglione*. In the hills above the city this is a picturesque resutauarant with superb panoramic views over the city from the balcony and the second floor. A perfect and good-value summer stop-off on during weekend randonees in the countryside outside the stifling city.

Osterias

€ Osteria Natali, via di Casaglia 62, **T** 051-589093. *Left fork off via Saragozza to southwest*. If you are up in the surrounding hills this bar has a relaxing garden perfect for tasting a pre-dinner glass of wine with *crescentine* and salami.

African

€ Adal, via G Vasari 7, **T** 051-374891. *Closed Mon. In Bolognina east of via di Corticella*. An Eritrean restaurant devoted to the cuisine of one of Italy's few ex-colonies. At weekends there are often poetry readings, live African music and Ethiopia, Eritrea and Somalia films.

Cafés

La Caramella, via Cadriano 27, **T** 051-505074. *Northeast of via San Donato beyond tangenziale*. A calorifc extravaganza – one of the best cake and sweet shops in Bologna serving local specialities such as *torta di riso* (rice cake) and innovative concoctions, as well as 24 types of chocolate. At lunchtime there is a buffet of salads and pizza slices, croissants – in fact anything you could possibly want.

Poco Loco, via Mezzofanti 18, no **T**. Located in a residential district southeast off via Mazzini, this Mexican ranch-like establishment is *the* place to go for brunch on Saturday mornings, where a feast of abundant and delicious self-service dishes will cure any hangover.

Around Bologna

Parma

€€€ **Parizzi**, via della Repubblica 71, **T** 0521 285952. Currently viewed as the best in town, offering a wide range of inventive and traditional dishes with impeccable service.

€€€ **Il Trovatore**, via Affo, **T** 0521 236905. Elegant and spacious, this restaurants serves up local specialties in style.

€ **Antica Osteria Fontana**, strada Farini 24, **T** 0521 286037. Mythical among locals, this authentic piece of local tradition serves inexpensive dishes and sandwiches in an atmospheric setting.

Modena

€€€ **Borso d'Este**, piazza Roma 5, **T** 059-214114. In a prime location on the magnificent square, this is currently viewed as the best restaurant in town, serving adventurous and traditional dishes with equal flair and flavour – at a price.

€€€ **Cucina del Museo**, via Sant'Agostino 5, **T** 059-217429. A tiny gem in the old centre with only six tables but a big menu of creative traditional and experimental dishes. Book ahead.

€€€ **Fini**, piazzetta San Francesco, **T** 059-223314. For a long time the most renowned restaurant in town and still serving delicious food with impeccable service in a nice Art Nouveau setting.

€€ **Aldina**, via Albinelli 40. Affordable and tasty food from all over Italy.

€€ **Da Enzo**, via Coltellini 7. Modenese specialities in an old-fashioned setting. Relatively expensive.

€€ **Santa Chiara**, via Ruggera. A chic resraurant with innovative dishes and local specialities.

€ **Giusti**, via Farini 75/vicolo Squallore 46, **T** 059-222533. Part of the furniture: a useful deli with a bar next door. Good sandwiches.

Ferrara

€€ **Antica Osteria delle Volte**, via delle Volte 37/a, **T** 0532-762033. In the medieval heart of Ferrara, this is a rustic and reasonably priced option with a good atmosphere**.**

€€ **Max**, piazza della Repubblica 16, **T** 0532-209309. Popular with a young crowd. Great and relatively light food with an extensive wine list.

€€ **Guido**, via Vignatagliata 6, **T** 0532-761052. Food has been served here for over 100 years. The restaurant's latest owner, Guido keeps a tradition of delicious regional specialities.

Imola

€€€ **La Volta**, via SS Selice 82, **T** 0542-5102. Refined fish specialities but also the full regional works in an Art Nouveau setting.

€€ **del Vicolo Nuovo**, vicolo Codronchi 6, **T** 0542-32552. *Closed Sun and Mon*. Traditional cuisine in a 17th-century former Jesuit school in the middle of the historic centre.

€€ **San Domenico**, vicolo Sacchi 1. *Closed Sun eve and Mon.* Considering the fact that this restaurant is considered one of the best in all Italy it is amazing you don't have to have won the lottery to afford to eat here. Should be your first port of call.

Rimini

€€ **Marinelli da Vittorio**, viale Valurio 39, **T** 0541-783289. Fun and busy restaurant in the centro storico. Great fresh fish.

€€ **Saraghina's**, via Poletti 32, **T** 0541-783794. Superior seafood in a cordial central setting.

€ **Acero Rosso**, viale Tiberio 11, **T** 0541-53577. Elegant with courtyard in summer in the old centre.

Bologna is the Italy that works.

Charles Richards, The new Italians

Bologna has a kicking bar and club scene. Ever since the city became a university centre, its students have needed to be entertained, distracted from their studies and inspired by alcoholic hedonism and hallucination. The drinking traditions of Bologna's down-at-heel *osterie* go back almost a thousand years and are still intact now, even if the venues themselves have gone a little more upmarket. Add to that historic vibrancy a present-day openness and an ability to absorb and experiment with new influences and you have a city that is more unchained than most in Italy. Music and original hybrid bar-cum-nightclub experiences to suit most tastes, persuasions and moods are on offer. A number of Bologna's clubs attract international names on the DJ circuit. Activity centres around two or three areas: kick off the evening in the Quadrilatero, piazza Minghetti or piazza Malpighi before the ritual of supper. Then move on with the crowds to the concentration of bars in either the university district or around via del Pratello.

Aperitivo time (1900-2100) is when everyone gets going, drinking tiny multi-coloured cocktails or *prosecco* and snacking on a wide selection of free nibbles that every bar provides. Then it's dinner time which stretches until around 2300, when you can again change venue for a *digestivo*.

Most of the innovative and edgy nightclubs are in the northwest of the city and just outside, while more traditional, boppy discos are to be found in the surrounding hills. Bars with English names are generally to be avoided. Some bars and clubs legally have to belong to social circles and you may be asked for a *tessera* (membership card) for one of the social clubs (eg ARCI). Usually if you say you are just visiting and leave some ID at the door you won't have to buy the membership which otherwise costs around €20-30 for a year. Clubs that don't require membership usually charge around €10-15. This generally includes an obligatory (alcoholic) drink. For a comprehensive listing of bars and nightclubs and for up-to-date information on who or what's on where, consult the excellent *TalkaBOut* English language monthly or the new bi-lingual monthly magazine published by the commune, *BOnews*.

Centre: piazza Maggiore and around

Bars

Al Calice, via Clavature 13, **T** 051-264506. *Closed Sun Map 4, E5, p256* A modern, neutral-looking bar specializing in fresh oysters at aperitif time, together with the appropriate tipple.

Balmoral, via de Pignattari 1, **T** 051-228694. *Closed Sun. Map 4, E3, p256* Formerly the gastronomic heaven of the Nuobo Notai restaurant, this has now been turned into an Italian-style pub – fun but rather less tasty and glamorous.

Café De Paris, piazza Minghetti, **T** 051-234980. *Open daily until late.* *Map 4, F5, p256* This is the hottest night-spot at the moment and also does light lunches (by Bologna standards). At night there are masses of top *aperitivi* snacks, plates of pasta, sandwiches, crisps, olives – which means it is packed between 1900 and 2100 on Fridays and Saturdays when the beautiful people come to cruise and the DJ cranks up the volume. Things calm down later and you can find a table in the covered outdoor section.

Canton de' Fiori, via dell'Indipendenza 1, **T** 051-267300. *Closed Sun.* *Map 4, C3, p256* In the ancient quadrivio where the florists sell their fragrant wares with a few tables outside under porticoes in summer season. Frescoes above the entrance depict three goods bestowed by mother nature on man: bread, wine and canapa with the inscription *in vina laetitia e cannabis protecta*.

Mocambo, via d'Azeglio 1/7, **T** 051-229 516. *0700-2030. Closed Sun.* *Map 4, E3, p256* Aperitifs for the chic with delicious spicy nibbles and generous glassfuls of your favourite plonk. Also do fantastic breakfasts with the famed, super creamy, *café crème*.

Rosa Rose, via Clavature 18, **T** 051-225071. *Map 4, E5, p256* At its quietest at lunch but still popular for a light snack, this place transforms at night with great crowds of sunglassed *fighetti* spilling out onto the narrow street with the gigantic appetizers on offer at aperitivo time. So varied and bountiful are they that you'll be hard-pushed to leave with an appetite afterwards. Currently one of Bologna's trendiest night-spots (you're either a Café de Paris or a Rosa Rose person) the bar is jam-packed in the evenings and the locals fall over themselves to be seen here. Take one of the laden carving boards and sit more peacefully in the street.

Bars and clubs

Northeast: the university quarter

Bars

Birreria Il Druido, via Mascarella 26/b, **T** 051-226757. *Closed Wed. Map 2, G10, p253* More than 150 brands of beer with good sandwiches and chatty bartenders. Open air seating during the hot summer months.

Bistrot Le Stanze del Tenente, via Borgo San Pietro 1, **T** 051-228767. *Tue-Fri 1100-2300, Sat and Sun 1100-0230, closed Mon.   Map 2, G9, p253* Set in the magnificent former chapel of the Bentivoglio, with tall stone ceilings and walls covered in 17th-century frescoes, this bar has one the city's most unusual, edgy and creative decors, very popular with young and trendy locals. Onto this classical background the owners have placed a mixture of futuristic, Gothic and 70s furnishings, from tall dribbled candleticks, to metal lamps and orange sofas. There are three contrasting rooms off the main bar, each divided by a secretive curtain. One is a dining room with a traditional menu served in trendy (small) portions. If its not taken, sit on the raised section where the altar used to be. The venue sometimes hosts classical music concerts. Cocktails are the speciality of the house. Internet.

Bottega del Vino Olindo Faccioli, via Altabella 15, **T** 051-223171. *1800-0200. Closed Sun.   Map 4, C4, p256* Recently restored this historic and centrally located tavern still retains its 1920s interior with dark wood furnishings, stylish chairs and the main bar area. A convivial place for the evening aperitif where in theory, in time-honoured ritual, the first drink should contain an uovo sodo (boiled egg) – not obligatory. Wine tasting evenings are organized occasionally.

Cantina Bentivoglio, via Mascarella 4/b, **T** 051-222 119. *From 2000. Closed Mon.*   *Map 2, G9, p253*   The heart of the Bolognese night-scene, this huge cavernous jazz café offers great wine and simple food and live jazz every night. The specials are always worth checking and are delicious. You can chose to sit down by the band and pay a little extra, or stick to the quieter rooms on ground level. Booking is essential for a Sat-night table downstairs.

Celtic Druid, via Caduti di Cefalonia 5, **T** 051-224 212. *Open daily. Just off via Rizzoli.*   *Map 4, G10, p253*   An Irish Pub with a name one would never find on the Esmerald Isle, but it does boast Irish staff and a happy hour from opening at 2030. This is the first port of call for ex-pat workers and the kind of place where everyone remembers your name.

Cluricaune, via Zamboni 18, **T** 051-263419. *Just around the corner from the Hotel San Donato.*   *Map 4, B7, p256*   This Irish bar is more Irish than most you find in Ireland. But its vaulted ceilings and rickety wooden furnishings and barrels (unusually unkempt for Italy) do a good job of creating a dark and smokily traditional atmosphere. It is usually packed, mostly with students and the atmosphere is kicking. A good place to mix with the young locals, watch sport on TV and for the homesick to enjoy a good pint of Guinness.

Contavalli, via Belle Arte, 2, **T** 051-268 395. *Closed Sun.*   *Map 2, H9, p253*   Odd but fun little *aperitivo* bar with art shows every so often. They also serve *bruschetta* and snacks in the back room.

Fluxus, via Goito 9, **T** 051-233199. *Open late Mon-Sat.*   *Map 4, A4, p256*   Groovy bar attracting the cool and the cross-dressing crowd though the venue is a gay/straight mix. Also stages audiovisual exhibitions.

Insomnia, via de'Giudei 8, **T** 051-261552. *Closed Mon*.
Map 4, C6, p256 Trendy bar open until late with outdoor
seating in the summer.

L'Antica Stuzzicheria, via Mascarella, no **T**. *Map 2, G9, p253*
Crammed full of interesting odds and ends and with extremely
genial staff, this is a bar full of dark intimate corners for clandestine
jugs of wine and plates of cheese with your *amore*.

Lido del Guasto, via del Guasto, www.universointerculturale.it
Map 4, A8, p256 Literally meaning 'waste' the 'guasto' is a
regenerated former children's playground built in 1970s which had
been lost to drug pushers. A manifestation of the creativity of the
Bolognese youth, this bar hosts a free-wheeling and apparently
improvized mix of post-modern fashion shows, art shows, and a
changing choice of music from piano-bar relaxation to drum 'n'
bass, all in the open air.

Lord Lister, via Zamboni 56, **T** 051-240886. *Map 2, H11, p253*
A lively English-style pub under the porticoes of the student
district with ranch-like sets of tables and chairs outside.

Moodys, via Mascarella, 84/b, **T** 051-249510. *Open until late*.
Map 2, F10, p253 With happy hour prices from 2100-2330 you
can't go far wrong for strong cocktails and loud music, with a
restaurant round the back in case you find you just can't leave.

Rose Selavy, via Marsala 5, **T** 051-271961. *Map 2, B7, p253*
Super-chic restaurant/bar. Everything about this bar screams
Lenny Kravitz from the zebra-print upholstery to the 'is that a small
creature?' light shades. A place to see and be seen, with famously
slow service.

Scuderia, piazza Verdi, **T** 051-6569619. *Map 4, B8, p256* Recently opened, this bar-club under a beautiful frescoed arch stands on the site of the former stables (*scuderia*) of the Bentivoglio family. Run by the Rosa Rose group it is a typically funky hybrid of cool grooves and tunes for young, trendy and beautiful locals. Occasionally hosts concerts and live music on the square outside.

X, via del Borgo di San Pietro. *Map 2, F9, p253* Very *fighetto* Cuban, Latin-America bar.

Clubs

Corto Maltese, via del Borgo di San Pietro 9, **T** 051-229746. *Daily until 0400. Map 4, G9, p253* Disco pub with a little something for everyone. Sam's happy hour goes from 1930-2100 with Milanese-style *apperitivi* in the form of huge free plates of pasta. The back room starts pumping up the volume at around 2200, and a mixed crowd of students and young professionals come to drink cocktails, play pool and dance the night away.

Kinki, via Zamboni 1, **T** 051-5875178. *Map 4, C6, p256* Designer kitsch and fusion funk and house for gay and beautiful straight people. Mirrors and vinyl decor under the Two Towers.

Jam Club, via Mascarella, 2a, **T** 051-221003. *Map 2, H9, p253* Much less of a student hang-out with Monday-night-is- rock-night for an over-25 crowd. Women usually get in free before 0100, but men have to pay all night. A small restaurant caters for midnight munchies. This is also one of the few clubs that sells cigarettes.

Soda Pops, via Castel Tialto 6, **T** 051-272 079. *Off via San Vitale. Map 4, D6, p256* Funky dungeonesque bar/club by the Two Towers with free entrance until late. Popular with students for its super-strength cocktails, the music has lately veered towards US rap.

Zoom, via Mascarella 60, **T** 051-241963. *Map 2, F10, p253* Tiny mixed gay/straight bar with occasional live music, and 'park' nights, where the bar is transformed with turf, branches, flowers and starlight into an indoor-outdoor kind of thing. Different.

Southeast: Santo Stefano and around

Bars

Alla Corte di Bacco, corte Isolani 7, **T** 051-237884. *Map 4, E7, p256* In the arcade complex just off piazza Santo Stefano this is a lovely little wine bar offering over 400 different labels.

Chalet Giardini Margherita, Giardini Margherita **T** 051-307593. *Open every day in summer. Map 3, G11, p255* This bar/café in the centre of the park by the lake is an excellent venue for watching the sun go down over an ice-cream or something a little stronger.

Godot Wine Bar, via Cartoleria 12, **T** 051-226315 (and **Godot Wine Store** on via Santo Stefano, 12, **T** 051-26187). *0800-0200, Closed Sun. Just before the seven churches. Map 3, G11, p255* This wine bar boasts a broad range of top wines and a range of delicate little dishes to accompany them. Open almost all day, it is a great alternative for a good breakfast, lunch, light supper or for a tipple after the theatre. Service is quick despite the bar's name.

Kasamatta, via Sampieri 3, **T** 051-224256. *Map 4, D6, p256* Typically inventive hybrid bar, cinema and nightclub, with a thematic evening every Wednesday celebrating different countries and cultures. Happy hour from 1900-2200, with cocktails, buffet of the featured cuisine and an original language movie. The music takes over at 2200. Entrance free to tourists or students on these days. For the event programme, check www.serateinternazionali.it

Maurizio, via Guerrazzi, 22/A. *Closed Sun.   Map 3, D9, p255* Small cosy bar packed with antique radios and Bolognese sporting memorabilia – mostly from the two local basketball teams Fortitudo and Virtus. A live jazz venue every Friday night, the bar is also open all day for budget sandwiches and snacks.

Taberna dei Frati, via Arienti 25, **T** 051-23 98 80. *Open late.   Map 3, E8, p255* Good for a quiet drink last thing in a street away from the bustle of the centre. Broad selection of beers and tasty panini.

Clubs

Baraccano, viale Gozzadini, (opposite the Giardini Margherita) **T** 051-301211. *Open only Jun-Sep. Map 3, F11, p255* Two or three stages for bands and entertainers in this private park, with tables and chairs spread out under the huge old pine trees and two bars.

Southwest: around via del Pratello

Bars

All'Inzu, via del Pratello 5a. *Closed Sun.   Map 3, A4, p254* Trendy bar with big screen.

Caracol, piazza Galileo, 6, **T** 051-222 610. *Until 0200.   Map 4, E2, p256* Mexican bar/restaurant with excellent pitchers of Margarita and a very small dance floor. Happy hour 1930-2030.

Circolo Pavese, via del Pratello 51/3, **T** 051-550221. *Until 0300 Mon-Sat. Admission only with the ARCI (p167) passcard; for sale on site. Map 3, A3, p254* A place to sip wine and watch experimental theatre and short film projections in the company of Bologna's would-be artists.

Farmagia, via S Isaia, 4/bc, **T** 051-6449561. Map 3, B4, p254
Packed and pricey cocktail bar with great decor and a good chef
offering a delicious and daily varying menu. Look out for the girl in
a silver bikini on a swing and the dancing Chinese dragon.

Habana Vieja, via de Grifoni, 5/2, **T** 051-584313. *1900-late. Map
4, F1, p256* Cocktails, Mexican tapas, Cuban cigars – this place is
Latino overload but fun. Thursdays is live music with visiting
'Cuban' bands. Lively at weekends. This is also the safest bar in
Bologna due to the proximity of the *Questura,* so if you have a taste
for off-duty boys in blue who know how to *Lambada*, this is
heaven.

Sushi Café, piazza Malpighi, 14, **T** 051-221 773. Map 3, A4, p254
Bar/restaurant offering cool relief from daily madness. Water pours
from ceiling to floor in a constant stream, while mellow lounge
tunes from resident DJs soothe the soul. Slip by for a Japanese beer
or full set menu amongst the foliage. Booking is essential as the
bar gets busy with *Beat Party* on Saturdays, gay night on Tuesdays
and international DJs the rest of the time. Spontaneous chair
dancing is highly probable as the small hours approach.

Monastero, via del Pratello, 66/a, **T** 051-557172. *Closed Sun. Map
3, A3, p254* Huge arched wooden doors and killer cocktails, this is
an upmarket little spot to stop and have a natter. Outdoor seating
in summer.

Riff Raff, via del Pratello 3, **T** 051-222888. *Open until the last
person leaves. Closed Mon. Map 3, A4, p254* A pleasant wine bar
with a good selection of international labels and good salads, cold
meats and cheeses too. Also mouth-watering Sicilian puddings
with half-bottles of dessert wine to accompany them.

Rovescio, via Pietralata 75, **T** 051-523545. *2000-0200. Closed Mon. Map 2, H2, p252* Owned by the Greek owner of To Steki, this wine bar has an international flavour both in its wines and small hot meals which are served until 0230. A useful place late at night and a nice little place for a quiet drink with friends.

Stranamore, via del Pratello 44a. *Map 3, A3, p254* Achingly trendy but with occasional art shows.

Transilvania Horror Kafe, via San Felice 134, **T** 051-556 444, (there's also a branch on via Zamboni). *Map 2, G2, p252* 3-D version of Meatloaf's *Bat out of Hell* album cover. Red lighting, shelve- loads of skulls and clear glass table-coffins complete with skeletons and the occasional snake. Interesting.

Viola, via Sant'Isia, 24, T 051-331 884. *Closed Thu, open 1700-2300. Map 3, B3, 254* Gentle Austrian-style café and one of the few places in town with seats and plenty of space to stretch tired legs. Also do great *aperitivi,* but close early.

Walkabout, via Nosadella. *Map 3, C5, p254* New happening bar very close to the English language cinema. Full of bright young things from the early evening onwards, there is also a quieter room out the back for those just wanting a drink and a chat.

Zelig, via Porta Nuova, 4/b (off piazza Malpighi) **T** 051-236737. *Map 3, A4, p254* Open every day for drinks or supper, this is the favourite hangout of Marco Jaric, the local basketball star. Run by a charismatic *signora* with unusual taste in clothing. Book ahead.

Clubs

Blade Runner, via S. Isaia 57d. *Closed Tue. Map 3, A2, p254* Discobar with downstairs dancefloor. Favourite with trendy locals.

Cabaret Voltaire, via Saragozza 15, **T** 051-6448426. *Map 3, C4, p254* Live music and dancing to various music according to the weekly menu.

Depot Hip Hop Gallery, via del Pratello 13a. *Closed Sun. Map 3, A4, p254* Dark, atmospheric designer bar with live DJ, art gallery and small dance floor. Gay on Tuesday.

HypeClub, via Santa Margherita, 7/2, **T** 340-3346980. *2230-0300. Closed Sun. Entrance fee. Map 4, E1, p256* Recent renovation has turned this popular venue into the hottest club in town. Mondays see cheap drinks for students and foreigners, Tuesdays are rock-nights with 80's classics, and Fridays are for funksters with the Sole Shaker parties: well-known Mellow Yellow DJs spinning the latest Italian grooves.

Northwest: around via Galliera

Bars

Auld Dubliner, via Cairoli, 2/c, **T** 051-243138. *Open lunch and evenings. Map 2, E6, p252* Large, spacious and friendly, this is the only venue in town (possibly in Italy) to offer genuine UK favourites such as shepherd's pie, fish and chips and baked potatoes with chilli. With an all-Irish bar staff this is the place to drown your sorrows in pints of ice-cold Guinness.

Borderline, via Riva di Reno, 110, **T** 051-221359. *1200-1500, 1830-0230. Closed Tue. Map 2, G6, p252* Large friendly bar offering happy hour priced drinks between 1830 and 2130, with a fantastic array of *aperitivi* snacks. They also have a full range of board-games out the back and are happy for you to while away the hours over a pint and a game of backgammon.

Chet Baker, via Polese 7/a, **T** 051-22 37 95, www.chetbaker.com
Closed Sun. Map 2, G6, p252 Jazz café with indoor seating and a
veranda in the summer. Open for lunch with Emilian cuisine, worth
booking ahead. Mussolini's son has been known to play this venue
with a host of *fascisti* packing the place out in advance.

Del Mercato, via Belvedere 13, **T** 051-237844. *Map 4, C3,
p256* Opposite the *mercato delle Erbe*, a nice place to relax with a
lunchtime glass of wine after the bustle of shopping.

Rumba, via Milazzo 17/f, **T** 051-63 90 792, www.rumbacafe.it
Map 2, E7, p253 Modern and trendy resto-café with live jazz and
blues on Wednesdays. Happy 'hour' on Thursday from 1800-2330.
The menu boasts a range of international and fusion cooking,
different from the traditional regional dishes.

Clubs

Cassero (ex Salara), via Don Minzoni, **T** 051-649 44161.
www.cassero.it *From 2300. Map 2, E3, p252* This male gay club
has moved underground to the docks and vaults where the city's
salt supply used to be unloaded and stored. Currently the coolest
cavern in town for all persuasions, serving up a changing mix of
house, fusion, and lounge funk. If only for its intriguing
architecture and history the place demands to be checked out.
With café, bookshop and beautiful roof garden plus views.

Kaos, via San Carlo 12, **T** 051-239964. *Map 2, F6, p252* An old,
traditional feature of Bologna's night scene. Disco and techno
music. Circolo ARCI (see p167).

Lilith, via Milazzo 24, **T** 051-6493006. *Map 2, D5, p252* House
music, '70s and '80s hits, R'n'B. Good for a Sunday evening apertif.

Link, via Fantoni 21, www.link.bo.it *Open from midnight. Free except for special gigs and international DJs. 10 minutes on foot behind the train station*. The ultra-funky *centro sociale*, formerly housed in a converted multi-storey carpark, has now moved to an equally cool and industrial venue. It is about to reopen with the same look and vibe – futuristic bar, enormous dance floor, performance art and live bands moving to techno later. Guaranteed to be *the* place to dance, chill and party.

Millennium, via Riva Reno, 77a. *Map 2, G5, p252* Fun, dark venue in a 15th-century townhouse, hosting art shows and diverse live music from French accordion players to little-known UK funk DJs. Also jazz and lounge music.

Spazio alato, via Lame 2, **T** 051-227940. *Map 2, H4, p252* Nightclub and exhibition space hybrid with one-off events.

Outskirts of Bologna

Bars

Birreria Amadeus, via G Dagnini 1, **T** 051-6234011. *Southeast of Centro Storico*. Over 100 types of beers from German lagers to strong Belgian beers and including exotic brews from New Zealand and Japan. Pizza slices, crostini and pastries are complimentary munchies. A little more expensive than most bars.

Enoteca Vini d'Italia, via Emilia Levante 142, **T** 051-541509. *Closed Sun. Southeast of Centro Storico*. The place to go if you are a wine connoisseur (or even a pretendu) and want to taste the full range of Italy's vast (and sometimes besmirched) choice of wines, interspersed by bites of salami, cheese and crescentine.

Kik Bar, via San Donato, **T** 051-511328. Northeast of Centro Storico. Prides itself on being the bar where you can taste every possible type and label of whisky on the face of the earth.

Clubs

Acquaria Club, via S Zampieri 2, **T** 051-6310801. Cabaret, live music and, more recently, lap-dancing.

Capannina, via San Vittore 29, **T** 051-581115. Revamped club out in the hills. Dance evenings alternate with experimental performance, live music and son et lumiere art expos. House music on Fridays; house, '70s and '80s on Saturdays.

Covo, viale Zagabria 1, **T** 051-508801, www.covoclub.com   In the 'lounge bar and disco' category this club is best known for the international flavour of the live sets with groups and DJs from the US and all over Europe performing a fun mix of '80's and indie stuff.

Estragon Balera Ska, via Calzoni 6, **T** 051-365825, www.estragon.it   *Wed, Fri and Sat 2100-dawn. Concerts start at 2200. East of centre, off via Massarenti*. Serves cocktails, sangria, wine, and loads of beers. Live ska, reggae and hardcore USA, popular with the student crowd. Famously hosted Gomez when they were in town, so worth checking the programme.

La Lumiera, via Sabbiuno 4, **T** 051-589182. *Summer club. Due south of centre en route to Sabbiuno*. Organized by the Rosa Rose group (Rose Selavy etc), this is essentially *fighetto* fun in the hills when the going gets hot in town.

Livello 57, via Muggia 6, **T** 051-271066. Italian version of a squat with jungle, reggae and ragamuffin. Bands occasionally plus pizzas next door. Popular with the student crowd.

Palazzo dei Congressi, piazza Cosituzione 5 , **T** 051-637 5165. *In the Fiera district*.   Concert venue. Tickets from Minella Rock Shop, via Mazzini 146.

Ruvido, via Maserati 9, **T** 051-6311892, www.ruvido.it.   *In the hillls due south of centre out of piazza San Mamolo*. Popular with the *fighetti* (the well-heeled crowd) this club and restaurant hosts 70's and 80's funk on Wednesdays, dance and cover bands on Fridays and 'Supergroove' on Saturdays – with other live concerts every night. Big dance floor.

Studios, via Massarenti 14.   *East of centre (bus 11)*.   Bands and dancing plus screening of art films. ARCI (see p167) members only.

Villa Montefano, via Volpino, 13 Budrio, **T** 051-6929587, www.montefano.com   Northwest of centre out through piazza San Felice. Booking is essential, as is a car. This 17th-century frescoed *palazzo* plays host to various classical, jazz and opera concerts, with the entrance price and membership card covering all the wine you can drink, and a light supper after the music.

Villa Serena, via della Barca, 1, **T** 051-6156789. Country villa close to *Lo Stadio* (an inexpensive taxi ride away) open at weekends with tables and chairs under the trees, free entry and cheap drinks. The top floor is home to art shows and installations , the ground floor has two bars with 80s-90s music. The basement has live local music until midnight, and dancing to poppy stuff until 0300.

Around Bologna

Modena

Vox, viale Vittorio Veneto, 13 41015 Nonantola, Modena, www.voxclub.it The best venue around for big name bands such as Coldplay, Morrissey and Suede. Book in advance over the web or at the ticketmasters in town.

Rimini

Rimini's clubs are famed for their size, international DJs and the outrageous show-dressing of their core clients.

Bandiera Gialla, via Covignano. Open-air raving in summer only.

Cocorico (Riccione), via Chieti 44. Italian techno in a glass pyramid.

Paradiso, via Covignano 260. Dance music with famous international DJs.

Pascia (Riccione), via Sardegna 30. Garage, techno and house, Italian-style.

Bologna has a thriving arts scene fuelled by budding and aspiring student artists and a very supportive local council. Particularly around the university district, the city is plastered with posters announcing the latest show, event or spectacle and flyers are constantly handed to you along via Belle Arti, via Zamboni and via dell'Indipendenza. The tourist office website is constantly updated with information on events and also has links to most venues' websites for further details. There are free local Italian newspapers, *CityBologna*, *BolognaBologna* and *Leggo Bologna* which provide space for and actively promote youth art. The council also publishes a monthly bi-lingual guide to the city's arts, entitled *Bonews*. The Bolognese are also very talented at improvising and converting the most surprising urban spaces into exhibition venues, be they car parks, wastelands or disused buildings. Many of the city's churches, virtually art galleries themselves, often host temporary exhibitions and concerts.

Cinema

Art house cinemas

Bologna has several art house cinemas and cineclubs showing films in the original language, sometimes with and sometimes without subtitles. In addition, there are often many short film projections in bars and as part of sound and light spectacles.

Fulgor, via Montegrappa 2, **T** 051-23132. *Map 4, B3, p256*
Lumière, via Azzogardino 55a, www.cinetecadibologna.it
Map 2, F4, p252 Film club showing classics in their original version.
Odeon, via Mascarella 3, **T** 051-227916. *Map 2, G9, p253*

Mainstream cinemas

There are also plenty of mainstream cinemas in the city showing the latest blockbusters. Tickets usually cost around €7 or around €5 for concessions.

Imperiale, via dell'Indipendenza 6, **T** 051-223732. *Map 2, F7, p253*
Medusa, viale Europa 5, northeast of the centre, **T** 051-6300511, www.medusacinema.it
Marconi, via Saffi 58, **T** 051-6492374. *Map 2, off F1, p252*

English-language cinemas

Films are screened in English on Mondays at **Cinema Nosadella**, via Nosadella 21, **T** 051-331506, *Map 3, B4, p254* and **Cinema Embassy**, via Azzogardino 61 **T** 051-555563, *Map 2, F4, p252* and on Thursdays at the **Odeon** (as above).

Emilia-Romagna was the birthplace of many famous Italian directors, including Bernardo Bertolucci and Michelangelo Antonioni, director of *Blow Up* (1966), who was born in Ferrara. Most famous, however, is probably Federico Fellini. His film *Amarcord* is a nostalgic account of growing up, inspired by his childhood in Rimini.

Comedy

As befits a rebellious city, Bologna has a long-standing tradition of satire, practised and honed to a fine art on countless lords and popes. Bologna is the head office of Italy's only satirical newspaper, *Cuore*, a weekly rag of irreverence, similar to *Private Eye*. Currently, one of the city's most acerbic and satirical voices is that of the novelist, journalist and playwright, Stefano Benni. Stand-up is less well-established in Italy, with comedy usually featuring as an element within a theatre performance rather than as an art form in its own right. The closest thing to Italian stand-up takes place at **Ruvido**, northeast of the centre at via Maserati 9, **T** 051-6311892.

Music

Bologna has a fine pedigree in both classical and popular music. Musicians such Rossini, Verdi and Respighi studied and composed here in the 19th century and, more recently, old-time Italian rockers, Lucio Dalla and Vasco Rossi, have called the city home. Bologna often hosts national and international rock and pop artists on European tours and, in recent years, has also become a centre for jazz, attracting residences by many international jazz names.

Teatro Comunale, largo Respighi 1, **T** 051-529011/051-529999 www.comunalebologna.it *Map 4, A8, p256* Bologna's famous main concert hall for classical recitals and opera. Very smart.

Rock concerts are held at the city's football stadium, **Stadio R Dall'Ara**, via A Costa 174, *Map 1, F3, p250* and at the **Parco Nord** in the Fiera district, *Map 1, B12, p251*

Jazz venues include **La Cantina Bentivoglio**, via Mascarella 4, **T** 051-265416 (see also Eating p170), *Map 2, G9, p253* **Chet Baker**, via Polese 7/a, **T** 051-22 37 95, www.chetbaker.com, closed Sun, *Map 2, G5, p252* **Container Club**, via dello Stallo 7, east of the centre, **T** 051-5311986. **Estragon**, via Calzoni 6, north of the centre, **T** 051-365825, for reggae, ragamuffin and ska.

Theatre

Bologna has a broad range of theatres hosting all types of performance from the traditional classics of Goldoni via the modern plays of Pirandello through to experimental and abstract theatre and comedies. The city attracts productions with star-studded Italian casts and also provides a stage for its own budding writers, directors and actors.

La Soffitta, Centro di Promozione Teatrale, via Azzo Gardino 65a, **T** 051-2092413, soffitta@muspe.unibo.it *Map 2, E4, p252* Modern and alternative cinema, dance, theatre and concert shows and workshops.

Teatro Alemanni, via Mazzini 65, **T** 051-303609, www.clubdiapason.org *Map 1, off G12, p251* This theatre specializes in shows in the Bolognese dialect or by local actors and writers.

Teatro Arena del Sole, via dell'Indipendenza 44, **T** 051-2910910, www.arenadelsol.it *Map 2, F7, p253* Classic Italian plays, usually dating from the 17th-19th centuries.

Teatro Celebrazioni, via Saragozza 234, **T** 051-6153370. *Map 3, D3, p254* Hip venue for Italian plays and musicals as well as some international hits such as Grease and Rocky Horror.

Teatro Dehon, via Libia 59, east of the centre, **T** 051-342934.

Teatro delle Moline, via delle Moline 1, **T** 051-235288, www.teatrodellemoline.it *Map 2, G9, p253* Modern, experimental and abstract Italian theatre in a cool surrounding.

Teatro Duse, via Cartoleria 42, **T** 051-225284/226606. *Map 3, D9, p255* Shows concentrating on local history and culture and abstract 20th-century theatre.

Teatro San Leonardo, via San Vitale 63, **T** 051-232280 /234822. *Map 4, D8, p256* A 'laboratory' for experimental theatre which also stages occasional classical and light music recitals.

Teatro Testoni, via Matteotti 16, **T** 051-4153800. *Map 4, off C1, p256* Shows for and including children.

Festivals and events

189

Celebrating has always been important for the Bolognese, as befits a people who regard every meal as a feast. In the past, the city was never shy about celebrating its independent spirit at each overthrow of a pope, tyrannical lord or invader. Any victory and its anniversary was a licence to throw a party. In medieval times, the streets would fill with jesters and revellers and jousts would take place. Bologna even had its own *palio*, a horse race around the piazza Maggiore, similar to that which still runs in Siena. The race, organized by San Bartolomeo, took place on 24th August every year, in order to commemorate the capture and bringing to Bologna of Re Enzo, son of Frederick II, after the Battle of Fossalta. Another famous festival was *la festa della porchetta*, held on the same day, at which a suckling pig was thrown down to the masses from the window of the Palazzo Comunale as a gift from the nobility. Napoleon failed to see the funny side of either festival and banned them both during his occupation of Bologna.

Nowadays, although this is still a generally festive city, the main festivals are those that follow the peaks of the religious calendar (Ascension, Carnival etc). There are also some artistic festivals organized by the council.

February

Carnevale Bologna's carnival belongs to its children who usually take part in a masked parade.

May

Festa di San Luca Bologna's main festival. On Ascension Day a procession accompanies the icon of San Luca down along the magnificent colonnade from its sanctuary on the hill, through the Porta Saragozza and eventually to the Cathedral of San Pietro. Here the icon lies in state for a week, during which time a series of powerful masses are held, before it is then returned to its home.

Matricole Today only an insipid echo of the animated and lewd 19th-century student initiation rituals.

Addobbi This ceremony, which has lost its medieval richness, takes place every Sunday in May and June. In celebration of the arrival of the Eucharist procession the city's churches adorn themselves and the streets in colourful drapes and lights.

Palio di San Giorgio (Ferrara) On the last Sunday in May, a medieval parade and horserace in the city centre.

June

Feste della Laurea Graduating is a seriously big deal in Italy. There are no city-wide graduation ceremonies, but you are sure to know about it if you find yourself in a restaurant of recent graduates.

July

Festivale dell'Estate (Modena) A mid-July week of festivities, including parades and extra-special meals, in honour of Este family.

July-August

Bologna Sogna or Viva Bologna This summer arts festival was recently initiated in order to stimulate the city in the summer when much of the population escapes either to the coast or the mountains. Open-air cinema and subsidized shows of all types go on all over the city and a temporary stage is put up in piazza Maggiore.

November

Baccanale (Imola) A Dionysian and calorific feast of special menus, tastings and general indulgence.

December

Natale (25th) As in most of Italy, Christmas consists of a family meal focused around roast lamb.

Vecchione (31st) The advent of the New Year is hailed by the burning of the old one, a ragdoll effigy which is set alight on the stroke of midnight in piazza Maggiore to the sound of crackers.

Shopping

Bologna is a shopper's paradise for everything from food and clothes to antiques and bric-a-brac. Not surprisingly for a university town, it is also well-stocked with bookshops. All of Italy's famous fashion designers and, of course, the local firms La Perla and Furla have typically stylish branches here, with prices still cheaper than outside Italy. And, if you want to recreate some of the amazing flavours you've been feasting on in Bologna's restaurants, there are plenty of delis and food shops for all tastes and waists.

Retail therapists should head for the via M d'Azeglio, via Farini and the catwalk-like Galleria Cavour arcade off Farini. Gourmets will have eyes bigger than their wallets and suitcases in the market streets of the Quadrilatero off piazza Maggiore.

Shopping hours are normally 0930-1300 and 1530-2000. Shoppers resident outside the European Union can claim tax refunds on their purchases. For more information on how to do this, contact Global Refund, www.taxfree@it.globalrefund.com

Alternative

Inde le Palais, via Marchesana 2. *Map 4, E5, p256* The coolest shop in town, set in the fortifications around piazza Maggiore. Clothes, furniture and various Indiana – like an Indian version of London's Momo. Bologna's hyper-cool Fashion Radio station churns out grooves in the basement to the slogan "Love the past. Kiss the future."

Mondo Bizzarro, piazza San Martino 3, **T** 051-229737. *Map 4, A6, p256* Books, videos and magazines relating to trash culture: fetish, occult, S&M, drugs… a taste of rebellious Bologna.

Soho, via Volturno 7, **T** 051-270568. *Map 2, H7, p253* Cool gifts and presents

Antique shops

You will find many, mostly quite expensive and stuffy antique shops along via San Vitale and via Santo Stefano.

Freak Ando, via delle Moline 14, **T** 051-271404. *Map 2, H9, p253* 20th-century collectibles – art deco, Biedermeier, Liberty – in a real shop of curiosities.

Books

Itinerari, via San Vitale 51, **T** 051-2960471. *Map 3, B11, p255* A quiet and well-stocked travel bookshop, also with some travel equipment for sale.

Libreria Antiquaria Palmaverde, via dei Poeti 4, **T** 051-232085. *Map 3, C8, p255* Second-hand and antique book shop, a favourite with writers.

Libreria delle Moline, via delle Moline 3, **T** 051-232053. *Map 2, H9, p253* New and old books, favoured by students and bookworms.

Libreria di Cinema Teatro Musica, via Mentana 1, **T** 051-237277. *Map 4, A6, p256* Specialist in performing arts books.

Libreria Feltrinelli, piazza di Porta Ravegnana 1, **T** 051-261392. *Map 4, D5, p256* This is the main branch of Italy's largest and best bookstore chain. Open late. Also at via dei Mille 12, **T** 051-240302. *Map 2, F7, p253*

Libreria Feltrinelli Internazionale, via Zamboni 7, **T** 051-268210. *Map 4, C6, p256* Just next door to the main branch, stocking English books and books in their original languages.

Libreria Mondadori, via d'Azeglio. *Map 4, E3, p256* Bologna branch of the chain, owned by Italy's largest publishing house.

Sala Borsa, piazza Maggini. *Map 4, C3, p256.* Within the former stock exchange building is an ample selection of books in many different languages.

Fashion

The local outlets of Italy's fashion designers are to be found in the roads off piazza Maggiore: **Furla**, via d'Azeglio; **Prada** and **Salvatore Feragamo**, via Farini; **MaxMara** and **Stefanel**, via Rizzoli. The gleaming **Galleria Cavour** shopping mall off via Farini often seems like a catwalk, with **Gucci** at no.1, **T** 051-262981; **Versace**, at no2, **T** 051-221016, and **Emporio Armani**, at no.9, **T** 051-238192.

Along **via dell'Indipendenza** are many funky shops with more grungy and experimental fashions. There are also a selection of stylish clothes shops between the bars and stalls of via

Clavature, including **Diesel** in a former aristocratic palazzo and **Stefanel**, under the arches of via Rizzoli. Prices are typically cheaper than in UK.

A.N.G.E.L.O, Vintage Palace, via Garibaldi 59, Lugo di Ravenna, Ravenna, **T** 0545-35200. *Map 3, D7, p256* The Italian second-hand clothes mecca where you can pick up Chanel, Dior, Gucci, Pucci, you-name-it for knockdown prices.

Bruno Magli, Galleria Cavour, off via Farini, **T** 051-6015011. *Map 4, F4, p256* Shoes for him and her, plus a few bags. The Magli factory is at via Larga 23.

Paris Texas Italy, via Altabella 11, **T** 051-225741. *Map 4, C4 p256* Dolce & Gabbana and Versace clothing and accessories at *dolce* (sweet) prices.

Speedshop, via Zanardi 298, **T** 051-6347194. *Map 2, A2, p252* Stock house for label-less designer wear.

Food

Al Regno della Forma, via Oberdan 45, **T** 051-233609. *Map 4, B5, p256* The nearest thing to Parmesan without actually going there. Great tyres of the stuff piled tantalizingly high.

Antonio Paglione, via Orefici 23, **T** 051-220657. *Map 4, D4, p256* Vegetables and exotic fruits, and magnificent truffles when in season.

L'Adriatica, via Drapperie 8, **T** 051-228695. *Map 4, D5, p256* Locally (Rimini) caught fresh fish.

La Baita, via Pescherie Vecchie 3, **T** 051-223940. *Map 4, D4, p256*
A shrine to all manner of pungent cheeses.

La Bottega del Caffè, via Orefici 6, **T** 051-236720. *Map 4, D4, p256* An aromatic array of different coffee types, ground before your nostrils.

Le Sfogline, via Belvedere 7, **T** 051-220558. *Map 2, H5, p252*
Considered some of the best freshly made pasta in Bologna, ready to go or beautifully wrapped.

Majani, via De'Carbonesi 5, **T** 051-234302. *Map 3, C6, p256*
Life is a chocolate box.

Paolo Atti e Figli, via Caprarie 7, **T** 051-220425. *Map 4, D5, p256*
All the region's different types of heavenly-smelling bread.

Salumeria Bruno e Franco, via Oberdan 16, **T** 051-233692.
Map 4, C5, p256 Mouth-watering and wallet-weeping regional specialities.

Tamburini, via Caprarie 1, **T** 051-234726. *Map 4, D5, p256*
A mecca of savoury delights: meats, cheeses and various preparations of vegetables to take away.

Markets

Celo Celo Mamanca, piazza VIII Agosto. *Thu only.* *Map 2, F8, p252* Antiques and various ageing jumble. The market's name literally means "I've got this, I've got this, but I haven't got…").

Giardini della Montagnola, *Sat and Sun only.* *Map 2, E8, p253*
The city's main flea market in the park. Bargain hard.

La Piazzola, piazza VIII Agosto. *Fri and Sat only*. *Map 2, F8, p252* Household and leather goods.

Mercato Antiquario, via Santo Stefano. *Sat and Sun every 2nd week*. *Map 3, F12, p255* Antiques worth bargaining for.

Mercato delle Erbe, via Ugo Bassi 2. *Mon-Sat 0700-1300 and 1700-1900, closed Thu and Sat pm*. *Map 4, B1, p256* Covered vegetable market, with fruit and fish next door.

Mercato Via San Giuseppe, via San Giuseppe. *2nd weekend every month except Jul and Aug*. *Map 2, F7, p256* Arts and crafts under the Two Towers. Negotiate fairly.

Piazza Aldrovandi. *Daily except Tue pm*. *Map 4, E8, p256* Food, fruit and vegetables.

Piazza di Porta Galliera. *Daily in winter*. *Map 3, F9, p255* Covered second-hand and antique book market.

Music/CDs and records

Bongiovanni, via Ugo Bassi. Specialists in classical music. *Map 4, B1, p256*

Casa del Disco, via dell'Independenza 39, **T** 051-234224. *Map 2, G7, p253*.

Magazzini Nannucci, via Oberdan 7, **T** 051-237337. *Map 4, B5, p256* Specializing in jazz, blues, soundtrack and world music. CD and vinyl.

Ricordi Mediastores, via Ugo Bassi 1-2, **T** 051-229604. *Map 4, C3, p256* Local branch of Italy's equivalent of Virgin.

Rock Shop, via della Grada 6, **T** 051-521551. *Map 2, H1, 252*
A quirky and attentive shop with an unusual selection of music.

Virgin, via Farini 13, **T** 051-276011. *Map 3, C8, p255*
Multi-floored megastore.

Supermarkets

Coin, via Rizzoli, **T** 051-238624. *Map 4, C5, p256* Bologna's main
central supermarket has the uncovered remains of the Roman
amphitheatre right in the middle.

Other supermarkets include **Centro Commerciale Via Larga**,
Galleria via Larga, northeast of the centre, **T** 051-532980, and
Esselunga, via Guelpha (corner of via Lenin), north of the centre,
T 051-6010727.

Wine

Enoteca Italiana, via Marsala 2, **T** 051-235989. *Map 2, H7, p253*
has the best selection of regional and Italian wines in town. Tasting
freely indulged.

Good selections are also available at **Enoteca vini d'Italia** (see
p179), via Emilia Levante 142, southeast of the centre,
T 051-541509, and at **Enoteca Gilberto**, via Drapperie 5,
T 051-223925, *Map 4, D5, p256* Avoid buying your wine in a
supermarket if you can.

Bologna is well-equipped with facilities for all the usual urban sporting pursuits such as football, tennis and swimming. From a spectator point of view, the city also has football and basketball teams that are well worth watching.

Set in the lee of the Apennines, Bologna is, perhaps more surprisingly, also a great place for outdoor adventurous pursuits such as cross-country cycling, kayaking, hiking, rafting and, in winter, even skiing.

As elsewhere in Italy, *il calcio* (football) is followed like a religion in Bologna. During Sunday afternoons in season, you are likely to see men walking in the park in silence, with a radio attached to one ear as they listen to the game. Bologna FC hasn't won anything since 1964 but began to feature again as a major force in the early years of the millennium, largely courtesy of national icon Roberto Baggio. Unfortunately, since the departure of '*il codino*' (the pig-tailed one) in 2003, the club's fortunes have subsided again.

Basketball

Palacanestro (basketball) is the only sport that gets a look-in after football and Bologna's two teams, Virtus and Fortitudo, are among the best in Europe. They play at **PalaMalaguti**, via Cervia 1, Casalecchio di Reno, southwest of the city, **T** 051-758758. You can buy tickets at the stadium just before the match or by calling EBC, **T** 051-555504. Competitive basketball games also take place at **Paladozza** in piazza Azzarrita.

Cycling

For cycling in the city, see p25 and p216. For mountain biking, head to the national parks, p102.

Football

Kitted out in red and blue stripes, Bologna plays at the **Stadio R Dall'Ara**, via A Costa 174, to the west of the Centro Storico, built in 1927 as one of Italy's first modern sports stadiums. League matches are held on Sundays and tickets for home games can be obtained from the ticket office, **T** 051-6111125 or from any branch of *Carisbo*, **T** 051-4211342, the local bank, which currently sponsors the team. Tickets cost upwards of €20 depending on where you want to sit.

If you're inspired by watching the professionals, Bologna's parks are usually full of young boys trying to bend it like Baggio. Alternatively, teams play in leagues around town at a number of clubs; try **Palasport G Dozza**, piazza Azzarita 8, **T** 051-6430411.

Sports

Golf

There are two courses within reach of central Bologna. A round of golf will cost upwards of €40 per person.

Gold Club Bologna, via Sabattini 69 in Monte San Pietro, **T** 051-969100, www.golfclub.bo.it *Closed Mon*.

Golf Club Molino del Pero, via Molino del Pero 323 in Monzuno, **T** 051-6770506. *Closed Mon*.

Gyms

Centro Sportivo, piazza Azzarita. The gym is open to visitors on a turn-up-and-pay basis. For details of the football club, Palasport, see above.

Palestra Refran, via del Fico 4, **T** 051-264596. Open to visitors on a one-off basis.

Hiking

There are numerous trails mapped out in the hills with red triangles but it is best to obtain maps and the latest information from the tourist office or the CAI (Club Alpino Italiano), **T** 051-234856. The GEA (Grande Escursione Appenninica) is a 400 km trail mapped out in 1983 that traces the mountain range from Liguria to le Marche of which you might want to walk a section. There are various mountain refuges at which either to stop and eat or stay over. Rifugio Citta di Sarzana, **T** 0522-431166 is on the GEA. The CAI has details of others. For information on the national parks around Bologna, see p102.

► San Marino Grand Prix

Named after the founder of Italy's most famous car, the Autodromo Enzo Ferrari, situated in the principality of San Marino, is arguably the spiritual home of the famous prancing horse *scuderia* whose fame was made by Formula One.

A fixture on the F1 calendar since 1981, the San Marino is Italy's most prestigious grand prix – perhaps because of the tax-free status the principality shares with Montecarlo. A tough and twisty circuit, San Marino has always produced exciting races. One of the most memorable in the last decade was Nigel Mansell, on his way to his first and only World Championship, screaming down the straight, bumper to bumper with his Williams team-mate Ayrton Senna, daring the legendary Brazilian driver to brake first and concede the corner. In 1994, the circuit and its high-speed Curva Tamburello (now a chicane) became infamous as the site where Senna lost his life, during a tragic F1 weekend that also saw the death of the Austrian driver Roland Ratzenberger.

In those days, Ferrari could hardly scrape together a point. But for the last few years, with Michael Schumacher at the wheel and Ross Brawn in the strategy room, Ferrari's star has risen again to dominate the sport. On F1 days San Marino grandstands are decked in scarlet and the roar of the *tifosi* is deafening – even above the engines – as their hero whizzes past hapless opponents, steering the pride of Italy to victory.

Skiing

In places the Apennines reach heights of 2000 m, guaranteeing good snowfall in winter. It was on the slopes near Bologna that

Alberto Tomba learnt to ski. There are over twenty well-equipped resorts in all, of which the following are the best.

Corno alle Scale/Budiara/Val Carlina 30 km of runs up to 1,945 m altitude. Downhill and cross-country skiing. 80 km from Bologna, accessible by train to Porretta.

Fiumalbo/Monte Cimone 16 km of runs, downhill and cross-country. Take the train to Pistoia.

Sestola 20 km of runs, downhill and cross-country. 67 km from Modena, accessible by train to Porretta.

Swimming pools

Bologna has a number of public swimming baths.
Bologna FC stadium complex, via Costa 174. *Daily 0930-1900*.
Cavina, via Biancolelli 36, **T** 051-247237.
Record, via del Pilastro 8, **T** 051-503311.
Silhouette, via Albiroli 5, **T** 051-237842.
Sterlino, via Murri 113, **T** 051-6237034.

Tennis

Centro Sportivo Record, via Pilastro 8, **T** 051-503311.
Indoor and outdoor courts for €6-€15, depending on peak or off-peak hours.

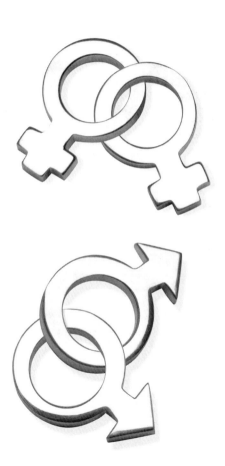

Gay and lesbian

In tune with its long-standing tradition for emancipated thinking, Bologna is one of the cities in Italy most open in its attitude towards homosexuality and has become regarded almost as a gay centre internationally. The city is the seat of the national gay movement and is considered to have reached 'the European level' of tolerance and understanding. The local council was the first in Italy to permit gay couples to apply for communal housing and Bologna was the first place in Italy to have a special *condomeria* (a shop – now closed – dispensing prophylactics and advice on safe sex for both gays and heterosexuals). It has not always been a smooth ride, however: Pope John Paul II once condemned Emilia-Romagna as the most degenerate province in Italy, partly on account of its gay tolerance. Rather than there being a defined gay scene, much of the overall buzz of the city and its nightlife is fuelled by the gay community. That said, there are a number of places around the city that are specifically viewed as gay meeting points. A good website is www.gaybologna.net

Associations

ARCI-Gay An organization of some 15,000 members, famously more than the Republican Party according to its President, Franco Grillini. It is based at Cassero nightclub, see below.

KGB The amusing acronym for the Komitato Gay di Bologna (contactable through www.gaybologna.net) is an internet-based meeting place, chat forum and association, which organizes parties, dinners, events and shows for the local gay community.

Ufficio Progetto Donna, via Santa Margherita 13, **T** 051-271457. A newly founded organization catering specifically for the lesbian community and also feminist interest, organizing meetings, events and discussions.

Bars and clubs

Cassero, piazza di Porta Lame. *2130-0200*. Sun night disco, Thu Les.Bo (lesbian) night. Also seat of the above ARCI-Gay gay and lesbian organization. This used to be under the Porta Saragozza where it attracted controversy since it is also through this gate that the holy San Luca icon passes once a year.

Da Renzo e Andrea, via L/ Spada 28, **T** 0349-5587077. Da Renzo e Andrea – a favourite place for a snack and drink among gays.

Gay Zen Café, via Mascarella 79, **T** 0338-2221993. *2200-0130*. A relaxed hangout for a quiet drink, frequented by both gay and straight males and females

Kinky, via Zamboni. *In winter only, closes in June for summer*.

Pachito, via Polese 47, **T** 051-243998. *2230-0400*. A small and dark nightclub frequented exclusively by gays.

Planet Girl, via Stefani, San Giovanni in Persiceto (*outside Bologna*). Not exactly central but a cosy retreat in the form of a bar-cum-club for girls only.

Gay-friendly hotels

Il Guercino, via L Serra 7, **T** 051-369853 (p127). **Hotel Marconi**, via Marconi 22, **T** 051-262832 (p127).

Gay-friendly restaurants

Amadeo, via Saragozza 88, **T** 051-585060. **Da Nino**, via Volturno 9. **Speedy Pizza**, via Saragozza 25, **T** 051-585203.

Saunas

Cosmos, via Boldrini 16, *daily 1400-0130*. **New Vigour Sauna**, via San Felice 6, **T** 051-232507, *daily 1430-0300*.

Useful information

The accepted and neutral word for 'gay' in Italian is *frocio* or alternatively 'gay'. The local radio station, **Radio Città del Capo**, on 96.25FM, has a gay hour 2200-2330 every night.

Rivalled only by food and fashion, children are the number one priority for Italians. Far from presenting a problem, you are more likely to endear yourself to the locals if you have children with you. Children are welcome everywhere. At *passeggiata* and *aperitivo* time they are paraded around on the shoulders of proud fathers. They are also taken out to restaurants and are allowed to stay up late with the adults.

In 2000, to coincide with their tenancy of the European City of Culture mantle, the council launched a special initiative called 'The City for Kids', which opened up galleries and theatres to Bologna's children and created workshops and exhibition spaces for them to indulge their creativity. This has left an important legacy, whereby significant concessions are still offered to children for entry into museums and galleries, differing according to age group. The development of the ex-Sala Borsa into a multimedia library (see p45) was specifically aimed at encouraging children to interact with local history and culture.

Bologna

Sights

Basilica di San Petronio (see p32) Children will be inspired by its sheer size and young curiosity is likely to be aroused by the astronomical clock.

Casa Isolani Check out the arrows stuck in the wooden arcade above this house (see p64).

La Specola (see p55) This is probably the most interesting of the university museums for children and the nearest thing Bologna has to a planetarium, housing telescopes and other complicated old instruments for star-gazing.

La Torre degli Asinelli The climb up might be a bit steep but energetic children will enjoy the view from the top (p47).

Museo delle Navi (see p56) Beauifully delicate models of 17th- and 18th-century warships.

Museo di Architettura Militare (see p56) Intricately carved models of armaments and toy soldiers.

Palazzo Re Enzo Let children discover and enjoy the acoustic effect at the crossroads under the belfry (see p38).

Activities

The **Giardini Margherita** and the **Giardini della Montagnola** are good places for a picnic or to let off steam on the lawns and among the trees. Bologna also has a number of swimming pools

and tennis courts that might keep art-weary children happy
(see Sports p206).

Sleeping

The more expensive hotels can provide cots and babysitting
facilities with enough notice but this is by no means a standard or
consistent service. Note, too, that the babysitter is likely only to be
a student earning extra cash rather than a qualified child carer.

Eating and drinking

Restaurants in Italy are generally very child friendly – even more so
now that smoking has been banned in most of them (see p221).
High-chairs are available on a limited basis and serving staff will
often spontaneously offer to entertain children.

Around Bologna

Sights and activities

Acquafan, via Pistoia, Riccione, **T** 0541-605709. *1000-1830,
Jun-mid Sep*. Riccione south of Rimini, is a swimming complex of
wave pools, children's pools, grassy areas and kids play areas. Then
there are always the beaches at Rimini itself.

Italia in Miniatura, via Popilia 239, Viserba di Rimini,
T 0541-732004, www.italiainminiatura.com *16km north of Rimini
on the SS16. Viserba* is a theme park showing pint-size versions of
all the famous sights of Italy from piazza San Marco in Venice to
the leaning tower of Pisa. There are also go-karts, a monorail and a
Pinocchio ride. Contact tourist information for more details.

Directory

Airline offices

Many airlines have call centre numbers instead of offices in the city. **American Airlines**, via Marconi 32 **T** 051-6492113. **British Airways**, **T** 199-712266. **Air France**, **T** 848878510. **Alitalia**, via Riva di reno 65, **T** 848865641. **Delta Airlines**, **T** 800-864114. **Go T** 848887766. **KLM**, **T** 02-58580245. **Lufthansa**, **T** 051-6477711. **SAS**, **T** 055-2382701. **United Airlines**, **T** 02 861831.

Airport information

Marconi International Airport T 051-6479615 (*daily 0630-2330*), **F** 051-6479719, www.bologna-airport.it
Forlì T 0543-474990, **F** 0543-474909, www.forli-airport.it

Banks and ATMs

Banks are open from 0830-1330 and 1430-1530 on weekdays. Closed Sat and Sun. Cash machines are available at most banks and accept Visa, Cirrus, Eurocheque and other international cards. The city's main bank branches are along the axes via dell'Indipendenza, via Rizzoli, via Ugo Bassi.

Bicycle and moped hire

Bikes can be hired from **Senzauto**, at the train station, **T** 051-251401; mopeds from **Ecofly**, near the station, **T** 051-245911. Prices start at €12 per day for a bicycle (*bicicletta*) and €30 per day for a scooter (*motorino*). A deposit of €150 or €515 respectively is payable.

Car hire

The following companies all have offices at the airport and also downtown, all along the northern end of via Marconi/via Amendola: **Avis**, viale Pietramellara 27, **T** 051-255024. **Europcar**, via Amendola 12, **T** 051-247101. **Hertz**, via Amendola 16, **T** 051-254830. **Maggiore**, via Cavoli 4, **T** 051-252525. **Sixt Budget**, piazza XX Settembre 6, **T** 051-255546.

Consulates

Bologna has consulates for a number of countries. **Austria**, via Ugo Bassi 13, **T** 051-268711. **Belgium**, viale Repubblica 13, **T** 051-505101. **France**, via Guerazzi 1, **T** 051-230505. **Germany**, piazza Calderini 2, **T** 051-273790. **Holland**, via Clavature 22, **T** 051-234115. **South Africa**, via Saragozza 12, **T** 051-331306.

Credit card lines

Amex T 06-72900347. **Diners T** 800-8864064. **Mastercard T** 800-870866. **Visa T** 800-877232.

Cultural institutions

Bologna has branches of many Italian institutes linked to different countries: **Italy-Holland**, via Castiglione 34, **T** 051-234246. **Italy-France**, via de Marchi 4, **T** 051-332828. **Italy-America**, via Belmeloro 11, **T** 051-262825. **Italy-Ireland**, via San Vitale 96, **T** 051-224372. **British Council**, strada Maggiore 27, **T** 051-221249. **Italy-Germany**, strada Maggiore 29, **T** 051-225658. **Italy-Israel**, via Polese 28, **T** 051-246063.

Dentists

Contact the main hospital (see below)

Disabled

Italy is a bit behind when it comes to catering for the disabled but Bologna is better than most Italian cities. Contact an agency before departure for more details such as **Accessible Italy**, www.accessibleitaly.com, or **Vacanze Serene**, **T** 800271027.

Doctors

Contact the main hospital (see below). EU citizens should take their E111 with them.

Electricity
Italy functions on a 220V mains supply. Plugs are the standard European two-pin variety.

Embassies
See under Consulates.

Emergency numbers
Police T 113. **Carabinieri T** 112. **Ambulance T** 118 or **T** 333333. **Fire T** 115. **Red Cross T** 118.

Hospitals
The city's main hospital is **Santa Orsola-Malpighi** on via Massarenti 9, to the east of the city, **T** 051-6363 111. Other hospitals: **Bellaria**, via Altura 3, **T** 051-6225111; **Maggiore**, Largo Nigrisoli 2, **T** 051-6478111; **Rizzoli**, via Pupilli 1, **T** 051-6366820.

Internet
Easy Internet Café, via Rizzoli 9, **T** 051-231074. **Infopoint Europa**, piazza Maggiore 6, **T** 051-203592. *Mon-Thu 0830-1300, 1500-1900; Fri and Sat 0830-1300.* **Informagiovani**, via P. de Crescenzi 14, **T** 051-525842. *Daily 1000-1300, 1500-1800.* **Sala Borsa**, piazza Nettuno 3, **T** 051-204400. *Tue-Sat 0900-2100, Mon 1430-2130.* **Sportello Iperbole**, piazza Maggiore 6, **T** 051-203184. *Mon-Sat 0930-1830.*

Left luggage
The left hand bulding of the railway station on piazza Medaglie d'Oro has both manned and locker left luggage services.

Libraries
The city's main public library is the **Biblioteca dell'Archiginnasio**, piazza Galvani 1, **T** 051-276811, open Mon-Fri 0900-1900, Sat 0900-1400. **Ex-Sala Borsa**, piazza

Maggiore – Bologna's new multimedia library. **Biblioteca Universitaria**, via Zamboni 33, **T** 051-2099360. *Mon-Fri 0830-1730, Sat and Sun 0900-1830. Main university library.*

Lost property
Lost property can be claimed at the lost property office in via dell'Industria 2, **T** 051-6018623, or at the railway station lost property office **T** 051-6302354.

Moped hire
See Bicycle hire, above.

Media
English and other language **newspapers** are available from kiosks at the station and around the main squares of piazza Maggiore and piazza Minghetti. The local newspaper is called the Resto del Carlino (named after the value of the change you used to get from buying a Carlino cigar).

Italian **television** has seven terrestrial channels with occasional good programmes making an appearance between the chat and variety shows.

Pharmacies (late night)
There is a large late-night pharmacy to the west of the station and also the **Farmacia Comunale** at piazza Maggiore 6, **T** 051-239690. If it is not open, a list on the door has details of the rotation of open pharmacies. For an emergency pharmacist or for delivery of medication, call the **Farmaco Pronto** on **T** 800-218489.

Police
The HQ of the Bologna carabinieri is at piazza Galileo 7, **T** 051-640111. Police emergency telephone is **T** 113.

Post offices

The city's main poste restante occupies the northern side of piazza Minghetti, open Mon-Fri 0815-1830, Sat 0815-1300. The hours of business for smaller offices are 0830-1330, Mon-Sat. A first class stamp costs €0.62, €0.41 for a postcard. Postcards arrive quicker if you put them in an envelope. Call **T** 160 for information on other rates.

Public holidays

1st Jan, New Year's Day; **6th Jan**, Epiphany; **25th Apr**, Liberation Day; **1st May**, Labour Day; **2nd Jun**, Festa della Reppubblica (Nation Day); **15th Aug**, Assumption; **4th Oct**, Festa di San Petronio; **1st Nov**, All Saints; **8th Dec**, Immaculate Conception; **25th Dec**, Christmas; **26th Dec**, St Stephen's.

Religious services

San Pietro cathedral, via dell'Indipendenza 7, **T** 051-222112. *0730, 0930, 1030, 1130, 1230, 1730*. **San Petronio**, piazza Maggiore. *0815, 0900, 1000, 1100, 1200 and 1800*. **Santo Stefano**, via Santo Stefano 24, **T** 051-223256. *0830, 1030, 1130 and 1230*. **San Domenico**, piazza San Domenico 13, **T** 051-6400411. *0900, 1030, 1200, 1800 and 2200*. **San Francesco**, piazza San Francesco, **T** 051-221762. *0730, 0900, 1100, 1200 and 1800*. **Santa Maria dei Servi**, piazzetta dei Servia, **T** 051-226807. *0930, 1100, 1200, 1900 and 2115*. **Santa Maria della Vita**, via Clavature 10, **T** 051-236245. *1900*. **San Giacomo Maggiore**, piazza Rossini **T** 051-225970. *0700, 0900, 1100, 1200 and 1700*. **San Luca**, via di San Luca, **T** 051-6142339. *0700, 0800, 0900, 1000, 1100 1200 and 1630*.

Safety

Bologna is a small and generally safe city, where the usual level of urban common sense will be sufficient to get you around without incident. Unlike other Italian cities further south, there is

▶ No smoking

Gone are the days when Italians blew smoke over your veg at the grocery shop. Surprisingly for a nation of inveterate, religious smokers, the Italians have, since December 2004, adopted the no-smoking laws that have been spreading through other countries in the EU. And, even more surprisingly, for a nation with only a cursory regard for its laws, the ban is being obeyed. In restaurants, Italians are no longer allowed their sacred post-prandial cigarette – although, if you are among the last diners in a restaurant at the end of the evening, smokers may seek your permission to light up. In public spaces, such as stations, airports and other areas, smoking is only permitted in designated areas. However, smoking in bars, cafés and, perhaps most importantly, in the piazza or on the street, is still very much a part of Italian daily life.

no serious problem with street theft, muggings or drugs and, although the city is full of dark alleyways and shadowy arcades, any danger is likely to be romantic and imaginary. The streets are largely safe to walk in by day and by night, alone or in a group. Bologna's male students tend to drink in large packs but are harmless; perhaps the only area where you may be accosted by a drunk is at the train station.

Student organizations
ARCI membership can be bought from any one of the clubs and bars belonging to this association, allowing entry to all other ARCI-affiliated locations. For **ARCI-GAY**, see p209.

Telephone
The city's dialling code is 051 and must be dialled before all numbers, even within the city. The prefix for Italy is +39. You no

longer need to drop the initial '0' from area codes when calling from abroad. For directory enquiries call **T** 12.

Tipping
Only the more expensive restaurants will necessarily expect a tip, although everywhere will be grateful for one; 10-15% is the norm. A few spare coins when you order a coffee might speed up the service. Taxis may add on extra costs for luggage etc but an additional tip is always appreciated. Rounding prices up always goes down well, especially if it means avoiding having to give change – not a favourite Italian habit.

Toilets
There are public toilets at the bus and railway stations and also just off the southwest corner of piazza Maggiore on via IV Novembre. Otherwise you can use the toilets in bars and cafés although it is polite to ask (you may need to get a specific key) and sometimes necessary buy a drink or sandwich first.

Transport enquiries
Airport enquiries   T 051-311578. **Bus enquiries   T** 051-248374. **Train enquiries   T** 051-246490, www.trenitalia.com.

Travel agents
Bigtours, via de Monari 2, **T** 051-239950/238411. **Hotelplan Italia**, via Santo Stefano, **T** 051-263601. **Viaggi Salvadori 1929**, via Ugo Bassi 13, **T** 051-225686/226493.

Background

A sprint through history

c1000 BC   First signs of human settlement around Bologna and the Apennines by the Villanova civilization.

c650-450 BC   Etruscans found Felsina on site of modern-day Bologna, then capital of northern Etruria.

450-191 BC   Felsina falls to the Gauls.

187 BC   Construction of the via Emilia begins.

189 BC   Romans defeat the Gauls and found the colony of Bononia. It suffers a great fire under Claudius but is rebuilt and enlarged under Nero.

AD 431-450   In the vacuum left by the decline of the Roman Empire, Bishop Petronius maintains the city under his bishopric and establishes the city's early boundaries.

476   The Western Roman Empire falls.

493-526   Bologna falls into the hands of the Goths under Theodoric.

554   The Byzantines take over under Justinian, ruling from Ravenna.

680   Lombard rule begins under King Liutprand.

774   The Lombards battle with the Franks. Bononia falls to the Franks.

1076-1122   The Wars of the Investitures mark the beginnings of a civic consciousness and the birth of communal power. The Guastalla Council, formed in 1106 frees Bologna from the jurisdiction of the archbishops of Ravenna. When Countess Matilda Canossa, the last representative of Imperial authority dies, self-appointed consuls take over and the *Comune* is born.

1088	Founding of Bologna's university.
1123	The first Bolognese consulate is formed.
1176	Bologna agrees to be a subject of the Lombard League.
c1200	Bologna is established as an independent *Comune*.
1220-1250	Reign of Emperor Frederick II. Conflict between Guelphs (supporters of the Pope) and Ghibellines (supporters of the Emperor) captivates and divides the country.
1249	The Battle of Fossalta. Frederick II's son, Re Enzo is captured and imprisoned in Bologna.
1278	Bologna surrenders to papal rule.
1325	Fierce rivalry between Ghibelline Modena and Guelph Bologna reaches a head when the Modenesi steal a symbolic bucket, *la secchia rapita*, immortalized in a poem by Tasso.
1348	The Black Death kills almost half the population of Bologna, then numbering around 40,000 citizens.
1390	Construction of the Basilica di San Petronio begins.
1400-1445	Bologna is governed by warring family dynasties, notably the Bentivoglios.
1506	Through a plot between Pope Julian II and King Louis II of France the Bentivoglio lordship is overpowered and papal troops capture Bologna. The city falls under papal control of Pope Julian II and the Bentivoglio palace is razed.

1572-85	Rule of Bolognese by Pope Gregory XIII in conjunction with a senate comprising 40 members of Bologna's noble families with hereditary senatorship. Bologna enjoys a period of great economic prosperity through its silk and hemp industries.
1630	An epidemic devastates Bologna, reducing its population from 72,000 to 59,000.
1796	Seven years after the French Revolution, Napoleon invades Bologna and frees the city from papal rule, suppresses the churches and monasteries and establishes French rule.
1797	Bologna is absorbed into Napoleon's Cisalpine Republic and becomes its capital.
1815	Battle of Waterloo takes place and Napoleon is defeated and dethroned, unsettling the status quo.
1848	Revolution and new power struggles rage across Europe. The First War of Italian Independence leads to defeat by the Hapsburg Austrians.
1859	The Second War of Independence under General Garibaldi is more successful.
1861	The *Risorgimento* and proclamation of the unified Kingdom of Italy under King Vittorio Emanuele of Savoy. Turin is capital of the new Italy.
1922	Start of the Fascist regime under Mussolini.
1941	Italy enters the Second World War as an ally of Germany. Mass deportation of Bolognese Jews.
1943	Mussolini is deposed by a coup and hung out for all to see in Milan. Italy signs an armistice. Nazis occupy northern and central Italy.

Aug 1944	Fleeing Nazis massacre 1800 resistance partisans at Marzabotto.
Apr 1945	The Allies liberate Bologna.
1946	The Italian Monarchy is abolished and the first Italian Republic declared. Centre-right Christian Democrats dominate Italian government for next 47 years. Bologna is the seat of the Italian Communist party.
1970	Bologna university is occupied by students in protest at government education reforms. The late 1970s and early 1980s re nicknamed the *anni di piombo* (years of lead) as extremists from the right and left reciprocate terrorist attacks.
1977	Bolognese students take to the streets in their local version of the 1968 Paris riots, protesting against creeping neo-fascism within the government and against neo-fascist splinter groups.
1980	Bologna station is bombed by right-wing terrorists. 84 civilians die.
1996	Bolognese University professor, Romano Prodi, leader of centre-left coalition L'Ulivio ('the olive tree') is appointed Prime Minister.
1999	Romano Prodi is elected Head of European Parliament.
Mar 2002	Marco Biagi, a Government Employment advisor is shot dead outside his home in Bologna. It is the first political violence in Italy for two decades.

Art and architecture

5th century BC
The most intact vestiges of Etruscan civilization in the area can be seen in the preserved settlement of Misa outside Marzabotto. Etruscan artefacts including bowls, tools and arms and architectural fragments recovered from the area around Bologna can be seen in the Museo Civico Archaeologico.

218 BC
Romans begin construction of the via Emilia between Placentia (Piacenza) and Arinium (Rimini) passing through what will be Bologna where via Ugo Bassi and via Rizzoli meet today. From Roman times until the present day motorway which largely follows its course, this road will make Bologna an important trade junction, central to its affluence and artistic and architectural richness.

AD 189
Founding of Roman settlement of Bononia (Bologna). The piazza Maggiore is the forum and central market place. This square and the grid of streets forming the Quadrilatero make up the entire extent of the original settlement. Only the narrow streets of the Quadrilatero remain of the Roman presence, together with a piece of the Roman amphiteatre found and still displayed on the site of the Coin department store on via d'Azeglio.

AD 402
Ravenna is made capital of the declining western Empire and enjoys an Indian summer of power and culture manifested in Byzantine mosaic art.

5th century
St Petronius confirms Bologna's boundaries and commissions a number of buildings, most notably the seven churches of Santo Stefano, inspired by a visit to Jerusalem.

727	Lombards capture Bologna and set about a number of urban embellishments, notably extensions and adjustments to the church complex of Santo Stefano.
1088	Bologna university is founded and with it the rebirth of the city's modern-day identity. The city expands in a typically concentric medieval way, with cobbled radial streets such as via Castiglione and via Santo Stefano.
1099	Modena cathedral is begun, marking a high point in Romanesque architecture.
1119	Among other towers, the present twin towers of Bologna are built. Around the same time the city takes on many of its medieval aspects, in particular the porticoes which are built in order to expand the city's capacity for the influx of foreign students. The second ring of the city wall, the Torresotto, is formed.
1221	The death of St Dominic, the founder of the Dominican Order, in Bologna leads to the construction of the church of San Domenico, a masterpiece of Roman-Gothic architecture and home to the famous and florid Gothic Arca over the saint's tomb, by Niccolo dell'Arca.
14th century	Taddeo Pepoli serves as diplomat between the papal forces and civic urges of Bologna and effectively holds power. He commissions the construction of many grand palaces along via Castiglione such as the austere palazzo Pepoli.
1390	The first stone of the Basilica di San Petronio is laid.

15th century	The patronage of the ruling Bentivoglio family bestows many embellishments on the city, most notably the church of San Giacomo Maggiore. After their overthrow art and architecture enjoys the patronage of papal envoys from Rome who support the arts and in particular the university. The Archiginnasio university building is commissioned, partly to stop the completion of the designs for the Basilica di San Petronio
16th-17th centuries	Foundation of the Bolognese school of fine art by the Carracci family of painters in rejection of Mannerism, who, together with pupils and followers such as Guido Reni, are commissioned to decorate many of the noble houses and churches of the city. Bologna becomes an alternative centre to Florence for art and a rich source of commissions. The city also enjoys great civic affluence giving rise to many Baroque embellishments and gestures, best manifested in the extravagant building of the covered portico to San Luca. The third ring of city walls is built and the city takes on the aspect it largely maintains to this day.
18th century	Napoleon enters Italy and closes many monasteries, divesting them of many of their works of art. Many monasteries are turned into storehouses. The canvasses, sculptures and frescoes are collected together in one place to form the present-day Pinacoteca. Simultaneously the Accademia delle Belle Arti is founded in Bologna and the main seat of the university is moved to its current location to unify its proliferating faculties in one area of the city as an example of a campus.

19th century	The Parisian fashion for boulevards leads to the destruction of many towers and medieval buildings for the creation of 'modern' avenues such as via dell'Indipendenza, via Ugo Bassi, via Rizzoli and piazza di Porta Ravegnana. Bologna's canals and waterways are covered over and filled in.
20th century	Birth of Giorgio Morandi in Bologna. The artist, who would spend all of his life in and around the city eschews grandiose avant-garde modernism and abstract art for a parochial and delicate attempt to praise and triumph the simple and everyday things in nature.
1974	Federico Fellini makes *Amarcord*, a film based on and set in his birthplace, Rimini.
1980s	The exhibition centre is built. Designed by Kenzo Tange, its towers, which in any other city would be ordinary skyscrapers, are meant to reflect medieval Bologna's architectural leitmotif.
2000	Bologna is elected one of seven European cities of culture to mark the millennium. A progressive local government ensures that Bologna's treasures are kept in a good state of repair and open to the public. The council supports many student art initiatives. A wing of the Palazzo Comunale is converted in a multi-media library aimed at bringing children closer to culture. Work begins on restoring the old port district into a cultural centre.
2004-5	The regeneration of the port continues with the opening of the Manifattura delli Arte. The city's medieval underground waterways are restored and opened to the public for cultural tours.

231

Books

Bologna does not generally feature as largely as Florence, Venice or Rome in the rose-tinted travels of 19th-century writers, dandies and Victorians on the Grand Tour. Mostly the city receives a cursory mention, focussed principally on its art treasures, but the following are all good reads. Bologna also features in passing in the portraits of Italy by Jan Morris, D H Lawrence and Edith Wharton. Many of the older texts are available as free downloads from Project Gutenberg at http://promo.net/pg/

Travel writing

Lord Byron, **GG**, *Letters* (various volumes, 1798-1822) Typically floral musings, extravagant statements and clever-dick comments in epistles to fellow writers and wordsmiths.

Dickens, **C**, *Pictures from Italy* (Penguin, 1866) Travelogue of incisive and refreshingly unblinkered observations and descriptions.

von Goethe, **JW**, *Italian Journey* (Penguin, 1786-1788) Beautifully written descriptions mixed with more abstract musings from the original Romantic smitten by Italy.

Morton, **H V**, *A Traveller in Italy* (Methuen, 1969) A gentlemanly and scholarly account infused with local detail and encounters with the natives.

Non-fiction

Barzini, **L**, *The Italians* (Penguin 1968) At times almost a character/nation assassination, all the more incredible in that it is written by an Italian. Possibly the most incisive piece of writing there is on the Italian mindset and the illusion that is Italy.

Jones, **T**, *The Dark Heart of Italy* (Faber and Faber, 2003)
An antidote to all the sycophantic prose about Italy's cuisine, climate, art and renaissance past. This acclaimed travelogue documents the seedy undercurrents of Berlusconi's Italy, often hitting some surprising nails on the head for those who seek to know the real 21st-century country.

Richards, **C**, *The New Italians* (Penguin 1995), A refreshing account of Italy and the Italians at the end of the 20th century that dispels the myths of Chiantishire and Bella Tuscany.

Fiction

Bassani, **G**, *Il Giardino dei Finzi-Contini* (trans William Weaver, Harvest/HBJ, 1977) Romantic novel written in Bologna but set in Ferrara. In 1970, the novel was successfully transferred to the screen by Vittorio de Sica, winning the Oscar for Best Foreign Film in 1972.

Newby, **E**, *Love and War in the Apennines* (Picador, 1983) Written with the wit and poignancy of a great travel writer.

Stendhal, **H** *Charterhouse of Parma* (Various publishers, 1839) Love, intrigue, jealousy and vanity set in the city of Parma.

Carducci, **G** The poetic works of the 1906 Nobel Prize winner are inspired by, among other things, his life in and around Bologna.

⭐ **Best**

Bolognese food books

- *The Classic Italian Cookbook*, Marcella Hazan (Macmillan, 1988) Exactly what is says on the tin – an indispensable starting point for Italian cuisine
- *The Gastronomy of Italy*, Anna del Conte (Pavilion, 2001) A bible to the cuisine of all regions, containing over 300 recipes
- *Lorenza's Italian Seasons*, Lorenza de' Medici (Pavilion, 2001) A beautifully photographed tome on the use of seasonal produce according to the calendar of Italian feast-days
- *The Culture of Food* (Comune di Bologna, 2000) Recipes and restaurants from the Emilia-Romagna area
- *Emilia-Romagna* (Gambero Rosso) Yearly Italian guide with recipes and restaurants from the Italian equivalent of Michelin.

Language

Local dialect

99% of Bolognese can and generally do speak 'normal' Italian but don't be surprised if in the markets or some of the more down-at-heel osterias you can't understand what's being said. Italy's regional divisions are as marked in its language as in its cuisine, and each region has not only very distinct accents but also, due to Italy's comparative youth as a unified nation, living dialects which are far from extinction. The Bolognese accent is distinguishable for its nasal quality and for a tendency to pronounce the letter 's' as 'sh – think Sean Connery with an Italian accent. Local phrases you might hear dropped into conversations are 'Bon allez', a vestige of Napoleonic occupation meaning 'basta' – 'enough!' and 'namo (short for 'andiamo') – 'let's go'.

Basics:

thank you *grazie*
hi/goodbye *ciao*
good day (until after lunch/mid-afternoon) *buongiorno*
good evening (after lunch) *buonasera*
goodnight *buonanotte*
goodbye *arrivederci*
please *per favore*
I'm sorry *mi dispiace*
excuse me *permesso*
yes *si*
no *no*

Numbers

one *uno*, two *due*, three *tre*, four q*uattro*, five *cinque*, six *sei*,
seven *sette*, eight *otto*, nine *nove*, 10 *dieci*, 11 *undici*, 12 *dodici*,
13 *tredici*, 14 *quattordici*, 15 *quindici*, 16 *sedici*, 17 *diciassette*,
18 *diciotto*, 19 *diciannove*, 20 *venti*, 21 *ventuno*, 22 *ventidue*,
30 *trenta*, 40 *quaranta*, 50 *cinquanta*, 60 *sessanta*, 70 *settanta*,
80 *ottanta*, 90 *novanta*, 100 *cento*, 200 *due cento*, 1000 *mille*.

Questions

how? come?
how much? *quanto?*
when? *quando?*
where? *dove?*
why? *perchè?*
what? *Che cosa?*

Problems

I don't understand *Non capisco*
I don't know *Non lo so*
I don't speak Italian *Non parlo italiano*
How do you say …(in Italian)? *Come si dice … (in italiano)?*
Is there anyone who speaks English? *C'è qualcuno che parla inglese?*

Shopping

this one/that one *questo/quello*
less *meno*
more *di più*
How much is it/are they? *quanto costa/costano?*
Can I have …? *posso avere …?*

Eating/drinking

Can I have the bill? *posso avere il conto?*
What's this? *cos'è questo?*
Is there a menu? *c'è un menù?*
Where's the toilet? *dov'è il bagno?*

Travelling

one ticket for… *un biglietto per…*
single *solo andata*
return *andata e ritorno*
does this go to Bologna? *questo va a Bologna?*
airport *aeroporto*
bus stop *fermata*
train *treno*

Gestures

Italians are famously theatrical and animated in dialogue and often resort to a variety of gestures in order to accompany or in some cases substitute words. Knowing a few of these will help you both to understand what's being implied to you and also to become more Italian during your stay.

- Side of left palm on side of right wrist as right wrist is flicked up **Go away**
- Hunched shoulders and arms lifted with palms of hands outwards **What am I supposed to do?**
- Thumb, index and middle finger of hand together, wrist upturned and shaking **What are you doing/what's going on?**
- Both palms together and moved up and down in front of stomach **Ditto**
- All fingers of hand squeezed together **To show that a place is packed full of people**
- Front of side of hand to chin **To signify 'nothing', as in 'I don't understand' or 'I've had enough'**
- Flicking back of right ear **To show that someone is gay**
- Index finger in cheek **To signify good food**

car *macchina*
taxi *tassi*

Hotels

a double/single room *una camera doppia/singola*
a double bed *un letto matrimoniale*
bathroom *bagno*
Is there a view? *c'è una bella vista?*
Can I see the room? *posso vedere la camera?*

When is breakfast? *a che ora è la colazione?*
Can I have the key? *posso avere la chiave?*

Conversation

alright *va bene*
right then *allora*
who knows! *bo! / chi sa?*
good luck! *in bocca al lupo!* (literally, 'in the mouth of the wolf')
one moment *un'attimo*
hello (when answering a phone) *pronto* (literally, 'ready')
let's go! *andiamo!*
enough/stop *basta!*
give up! *dai!*
I like … *mi piace …*
how's it going? (well, thanks) *come va?* (bene, grazie)
how are you? *come sta/stai?* (polite/informal)

Time

morning *mattina*
afternoon *pommeriggio*
evening *sera*
night *notte*
soon *presto/fra poco*
later *più tardi*
What time is it? *Che ore sono?*
today/tomorrow/yesterday *oggi/domani/ieri*

Check out...

www...

Index

Credits

Footprint credits
Editors: Sophie Blacksell, Julius Honnor
Map editor: Sarah Sorensen
Picture editor: Claire Benison

Publisher: Patrick Dawson
Series created by: Rachel Fielding
In-house cartography: Robert Lunn,
Claire Benison, Kevin Feeney, Thom
Wickes, Esther Monzón

Design: Mytton Williams
Maps: Footprint Handbooks Ltd

Photography credits
Front cover: Alamy (Chiesa di San
Francesco)
Inside: Alamy (colour section),
Julius Honnor (black and white)
Generic images: John Matchett
Back cover: Alamy (Mercato di Mezzo)

Print
Manufactured in Italy by LegoPrint
Pulp from sustainable forests.

Every effort has been made to ensure
that the facts in this pocket guide are
accurate. However the author and
publishers cannot accept responsibility
for any loss, injury or inconvenience
sustained as a result of information or
advice contained in this guide. Hotel
and restaurant codes should only be
taken as a guide to the prices and
facilities offered by the establishment.
It is at the discretion of the owners to
vary them from time to time.

Publishing information
Footprint Bologna
2nd edition
Text and maps © Footprint Handbooks Ltd
April 2005

ISBN 1 904777 41 4
CIP DATA: a catalogue record for this book
is available from the British Library

® Footprint Handbooks and the Footprint
mark are a registered trademark of
Footprint Handbooks Ltd

Published by Footprint
6 Riverside Court
Lower Bristol Road
Bath, BA2 3DZ, UK
T +44 (0)1225 469141
F +44 (0)1225 469461
discover@footprintbooks.com
www.footprintbooks.com

Distributed in the USA by
Publishers Group West

Publishing stuff

Complete title list

Backpacker guides

Belize, Guatemala &
   Southern Mexico
Patagonia
Peru, Bolivia & Ecuador

Lifestyle guides

Surfing Britain
Surfing Europe

There are many more Footprint handbooks and pocket guides in the pipeline. In addition, Footprint has recently launched two new series of full-colour guides. The Lifestyle series was launched in 2004, with the publication of *Surfing Europe*, and early 2005 saw the publication of the first Backpacker titles. To keep up to date with new releases, check out the Footprint website, www.footprintbooks.com

Mail order

Footprint travel guides are available worldwide in bookshops and on-line. They can also be ordered directly from us in Bath, via our website www.footprintbooks.com or from 6 Riverside Court, Lower Bristol Road, Bath, BA2 3DZ, UK

Footprint feedback

We try as hard as we can to make each Footprint guide as up to date as possible but, of course, things always change. If you want to let us know about your experiences – good, bad or ugly – then, don't delay, go to www.footprintbooks.com and send in your comments.

What the papers say...

"Superstylish travel guides –perfect for short break addicts."
Harvey Nichols magazine

"If 'the essence of real travel' is what you have been secretly yearning for all these years, then Footprint are the guides for you."
Under 26 magazine

"Who should pack Footprint? – readers who want to escape the crowd."
The Observer

"Footprint can be depended on for accurate travel information and for imparting a deep sense of respect for the lands and people they cover."
World News

"The guides for intelligent, independently-minded souls of any age or budget."
Indie Traveller

"I carried the South American Handbook from Cape Horn to Cartagena and consulted it every night for two and a half months. I wouldn't do that for anything else except my hip flask."
Michael Palin, BBC Full Circle

For a different view…
choose a Footprint

Over 100 Footprint travel guides
Covering more than 150 of the world's most exciting countries
and cities in Latin America, the Caribbean, Africa, Indian
sub-continent, Australasia, North America, Southeast Asia,
the Middle East and Europe.

Discover so much more…
The finest writers. In-depth knowledge. Entertaining and accessible.
Critical restaurant and hotels reviews. Lively descriptions of all the
attractions. Get away from the crowds.

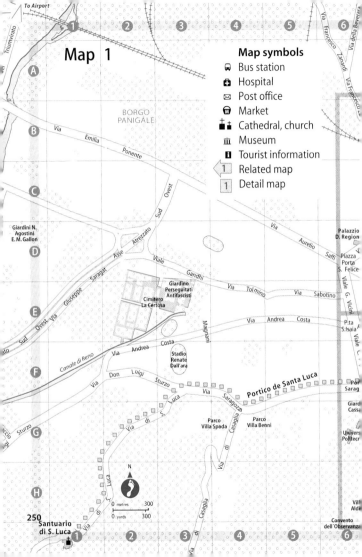

Map 1

To Airport

Triumvirato

Via Emilia Ponente

BORGO PANIGALE

Via Sud Ovest Atrezzato

Giardini N. Agostini E. M. Gallon

Via Asse

Via Giuseppe Saragat

Via Sud Ovest

Canale di Reno

Viale

Via Gandhi

Giardino Perseguitati Antifascisti

Cimitero La Certosa

Via Andrea Costa

Via Tolmino

Via Sabotino

Via Andrea Costa

Via Magnani

Via Andrea Costa

Stadio Renate Dall'ara

Via Don Luigi Sturzo

Via Saragozza

Via Saragozza

Portico de Santa Luca

Via S. Luca

Via di S. Luca

Via di Casaglia

Parco Villa Spada

Parco Villa Benni

Via di Casaglia

Sturzo

Via Aurelio Saffi

Palazzio D. Region

Piazza Porta S. Felice

Viale G. Vicini

P.ta S.Isaia

Viale

Por Sarag

Giard Cassa

Univers Politecn

Vill Ald

Santuario di S. Luca **250**

Convento dell'Osservanza

N

0 metres 300
0 yards 300

Map symbols

🚌 Bus station
✚ Hospital
✉ Post office
🏪 Market
⛪ Cathedral, church
🏛 Museum
🛈 Tourist information
◁1 Related map
1 Detail map

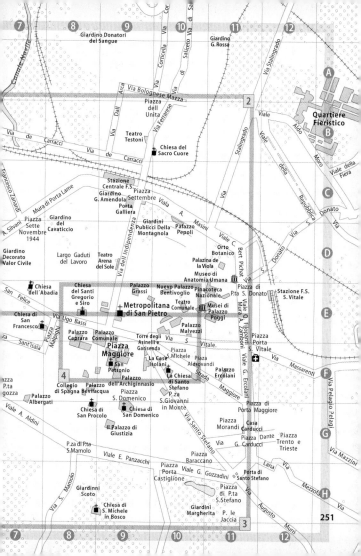

Giardino Donatori
del Sangue

Giardino
G. Rossa

A

Quartiere
Fieristico

B

Canale Navile

Via Corticella

Via di Saliceto

Via S

Via Stalingrado

Viale

Aldo

Moro

Viale

della

Repubblica

Viale
della
Fiera

2

Via Bolognese Mazza

Via Dall'Arca

Via Ferrarese

Piazza
dell'
Unità

Via Bologne

Teatro
Testoni

Chiesa del
Sacro Cuore

Via
de Carracci

Via
de Carracci

C

Via A. Silvani

Francesco Zanardi

Mura di Porta Lame

Stazione
Centrale F.S.

Piazza
Settembre

Giardino
G. Amendola
Porta
Galliera

Via XX

Via del Indipendenza

Giardini
Publicci Della
Montagnola

A. Masini

Palazzo
Pepoli

Via C.

Via Bert. Pichat

Donato

Via
Donato

D

Piazza
Sette Novembre
1944

Giardino
del
Cavaticcio

Largo Gaduti
del Lavoro

Teatro
Arena
del Sole

Orto
Botanico

Palazina de
la Viola

Museo di
Anatomia Umana

S

S

Giardino
Decorato
Valor Civile

Chiesa
dell'Abadia

Chiesa
del Santi
Gregorio
e Siro

Palazzo
Grassi

Nuevo Palazzo
Bentivoglio

Pinacoteca
Nazionale

P.ta S. Donato

Stazione F.S.
S. Vitale

E

Chiesa di
San
Francesco

Via Ugo Bassi

Palazzo
Caprara

Palazzo
Comunale

Metropolitana
di San Pietro

Teatro
Comunale

Musei di
Palazzo
Poggi

Via Fiopanti

Mura A. Zamboni

Piazza
Porta
S. Vitale

Sant'Isaia

Piazza
Malpighi

Piazza
Maggiore

Torre degli
Asinelli e
Gatisenda

Palazzo
Malvezzi

Via

S

Via Vitale.

Via G. Ercolani

Via Massarenti

F

zza
P.ta
gozza

Palazzo
Albergati

4

Collegio
di Spagna

Palazzo
Bevilacqua

San
Petronio

Palazzo
dell'Archiginnasio

La Case
Isolani

La Chiesa
di Santo
Stefano

Piazza
S.Michele

Piazza
Aldovandi

Palazzo
Ercolani

Strada
Maggiore

Piazza di
Porta Maggiore

Via Pelagio Pelagi

G

Via A. Aldini

Chiesa di
San Procolo

Chiesa di
San Domenico

Piazza
S. Domenico

Il Palazzo di
Giustizia

P.za
S.Giovanni
in Monte

Via Santo Stefano

Piazza
Morandi

Casa
Carducci

Piazza Dante
G. Carducci

Piazza
Trento e
Trieste

Via Mazzini

Via S. Mamolo

P.za di P.ta
S.Mamolo

Viale E. Panzacchi

Piazza
Porta
Castiglione

Viale G. Gozzadini

Piazza
Baraccano

Porta di
Santo Stefano

Via Lana

Via Augusto

Via Mezzofa

H

Giardini
Scoto

Chiesa di
S. Michele
in Bosco

Piazza di P.ta
S.Stefano

Giardini
Margherita

P. le
Jaccia

Murri

Via

251

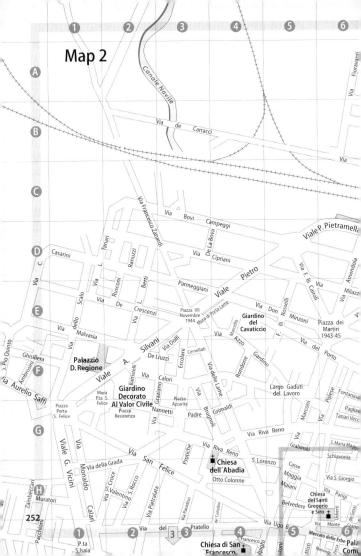

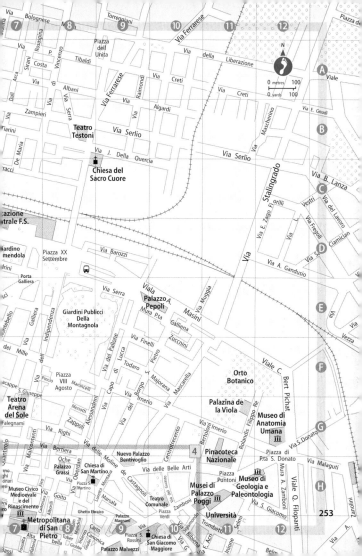

253

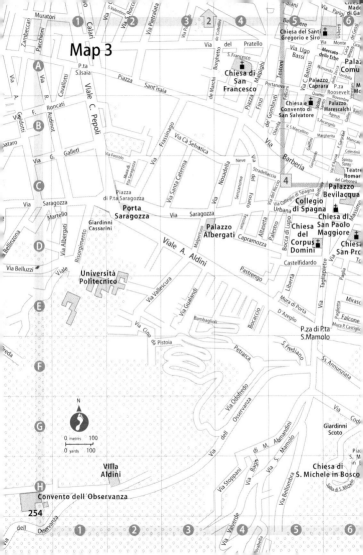

Map 3

Labels and streets (top area)

Muratori · Pacchioni · Zamboccari · Calari · Via · S. Valentino · Via Rocco · Via Pietralata · Via P.za · del Collelini · 2 · Via Parigi · Mad Gé

Chiesa del Santi Gregorio e Siro

A · P.ta S.Isaia · Via R. · Cavallotti · Piazza · Sant'Isaia · S. Francesco · del · Pratello · Via · Testoni · Mercato delle Erbe · Monte · di Ga · Palazz · Comu

Via Borghetto · de Marchi · S. Francesco · **Chiesa di San Francesco** · Via Ugo Bassi · P.za Roosevelt

B · F. · Vigidotti · Roncati · Ardinoi · Viale C. Pepoli · Piazza Finzi · Portanova · Palazzo Caprara · Raimondo de Terribilia · Via C. Battisti · P.za Roosevelt · Palazzo Marescalchi · Mo

Cataro · Via · G. · Galletti · Via Cà Selvatica · Via Frassinago · Via Foscolo · Mura di P.za Saragozza · Neve · Via Nosadella · Stradellaccio · Via S.Marcellino · S.Arcangelo · Chiesa e Convento di San Salvatore · Agresti · Margherita · Maescalc

C · Via · Saragozza · Piazza di P.ta Saragozza · Via Santa Caterina · Via · Sanzanome · Senzanome · Via delle Tovaglie · Barberia · Gaffini · Gargnolo · Spirito Santo · Celestini · Celestini · Teatro Romar · del Carbone

Martello · **Porta Saragozza** · Via Saragozza · Collegio di Spagna · **Palazzo Bevilacqua**

D · Via Albergati · Giardini Cassarini · Risorgimento · Viale A. Aldini · **Palazzo Albergati** · Capramozza · Altaseta · Palestro · Via del Lupo · Bocca di Lupo · Urbana · **Collegio di Spagna** · **Chiesa del Corpus Domini** · **Chiesa di San Paolo Maggiore** · **Chiesa San Pro**

Via Bellinzona · Via Belluzzi · Castelfidardo · Pastrengo · Teglipietre · Via · Paglia · Chiesa San To

E · **Università Politecnico** · Via Vallescura · Via Guabandi · Bocaccio · Mura di Porta · Libertà · Mura P.Castiglio · Falcone · Mirasc

Via · Viale · Bambaglioli · Via Cino da Pistoia · D'Azeglio · P.za di P.ta S.Mamolo

F · Petrarca · S. Frediano · Ss. Annunziata

G · Via Oddfredo · Osservanza · Via dell' · Via Bagni di M. Aframandini · Via S. Mamolo · Via Codi · Giardini Scoto

0 metres 100 · 0 yards 100 · N

Via Stoppani · Via · Bagni · Via Valverde · Via S. Mamolo · Via Bellombra · **Chiesa di S. Michele in Bosco** · Salita di S.Michele

H · **Villa Aldini** · **Convento dell'Observanza**

254

Via · dell' · Osservanza · Rosabella

Grid reference numbers

1 · 2 · 3 · 3 · 2 · 4 · 5 · 6 (top)

4 (middle)

1 · 2 · 3 · 4 · 5 · 6 (bottom)

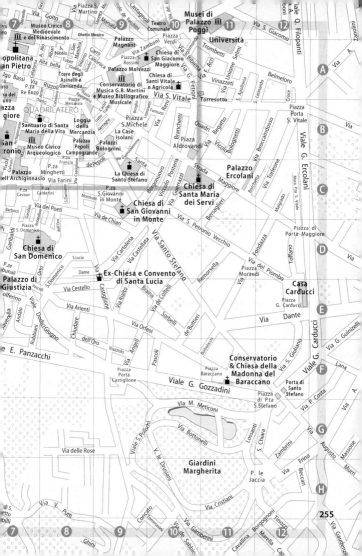

Via Goito
Via S. Martino
Via Marsala
Via Castiglione
Via S. Giacomo

⑦
⑧
⑨
⑩
⑪
⑫

Musei di Palazzo Poggi

Università

Museo Civico Medioevale e del Rinascimento

Ghetto Ebraico

Teatro Comunale

Piazza Verdi

Palazzo Magnani

Chiesa di San Giacomo Maggiore

Trombetti

Metropolitana San Pietro

Torre degli Asinelli e Garisenda

Piazza S. Rossini

Palazzo Malvezzi

Chiesa di Santi Vitale e Agricola

Conservatorio di Musica G.B. Martini e Museo Bibliografico Musicale

Via S. Vitale

Torresotto

QUADRILATERO

Piazza S.Michele

La Case Isolani

Bianchetti

Piazza Porta S. Vitale

Santuario di Santa Maria della Vita

Loggia della Mercanzia

Palazzo Pepoli Campograndi

Piazza Aldrovandi

A

B

Museo Civico Archeologico

Palazzi Bolognini

Santa

Palazzo Ercolani

Palazzo dell'Archiginnasio

La Chiesa di Santo Stefano

Strada Maggiore

Chiesa di Santa Maria dei Servi

C

Via Farini

Piazza Cavour

Monticelli

P.za S.Giovanni in Monte

Chiesa di San Giovanni in Monte

Bersaglieri

Via S. Petronio Vecchio

Piazza di Porta Maggiore

D

Via de' Poeti

Via de Chiari

Via Santo Stefano

Rimorsella

Via del Piombo

Piazza G. Morandi

Casa Carducci

Piazza G. Carducci

E

Chiesa di San Domenico

S.Lucia

Dame

Ex-Chiesa e Convento di Santa Lucia

Via Cartoleria

Via Castellata

Via Rialto

Via de' Coltelli

Braina

Via Dante

Palazzo di Giustizia

Via Cestello

Via Arienti

Via Orfeoi

Via de' Buttieri

Sorbelli

Viale G. Carducci

F

Conservatorio & Chiesa della Madonna del Baraccano

Porta di Santo Stefano

Via E. Panzacchi

Chiudare

dell'Oro

Viazzolo

Angeli

Pascoli

Viale G. Gozzadini

Piazza Baraccano

Piazza di P.ta S.Stefano

G

Via delle Rose

Viale S. Policini

Via M. Meticoni

Via Bottonelli

S. Chiara

Giardini Margherita

P. le Jaccia

H

di S. detto milli

Via V. Putti

Via Cristiani

Via de Sabbio

255

⑦
⑧
⑨
⑩
⑪
⑫

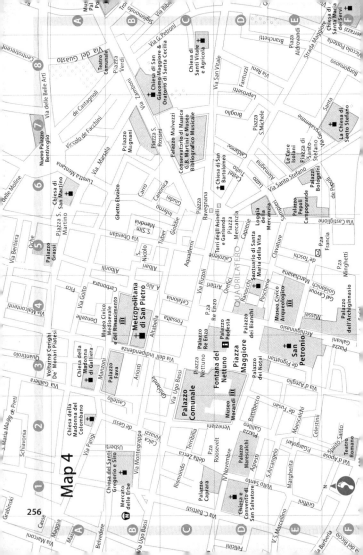